NORMS AND PRACTICES

Norms and Practices

JAMES D. WALLACE

CORNELL UNIVERSITY PRESS

ITHACA AND LONDON

First published 2009 by Cornell University Press

Printed in the United States of America

Library of Congress Cataloging-in-Publication Data

Wallace, James D., 1937–
   Norms and practices / James D. Wallace.
     p.   cm.
   Includes bibliographical references and index.
   ISBN 978-0-8014-4719-8 (cloth : alk. paper)
    1. Normativity (Ethics)   2. Practice (Philosophy)   3. Social norms—Philosophy.   1. Title.
   BJ1458.3W34 2009
   170—dc22
                                          2008022865

Cloth printing   10 9 8 7 6 5 4 3 2 1

To my children
David and Amy

Contents

Preface

This book continues the development of ideas about ethics and philosophical methodology that I began more than two decades ago. One reader described the work as "far out of the mainstream," and it is likely that many readers will find that description apt. I did not set out to stray; the ideas took over, and I followed where they led. I say this in the way of preface, though, not of apology.

Earlier versions of some of the material in this book were presented to various professional audiences, and their reactions helped shape the present version. A portion of Chapter 3 is reprinted by permission from "Social Artifacts and Ethical Criticism" in *Teaching Ethics*, Volume 1, Number 1 – March 2001. I am grateful to Frederick Kaufman for comments. Chapter 5, "Virtues of Benevolence and Justice," is a substantially revised version of an essay that appeared in D. Carr and J. Steutel, *Virtue Ethics and Moral Education* (London: Routledge, 1999). Robert McKim was kind enough to give me detailed comments on the earlier version. Chapter 2 appeared in K. Westphal, ed., *Pragmatism, Reason, and Norms* (New York: Fordham University Press, 1998), under the title "The Spirit of the Enterprise." An earlier version of Chapter 1 was delivered as the 2005 Humanities Lecture at the University of Illinois at Urbana-Champaign. Gary Ebbs convinced me of the need for some substantial revisions in this material. David Bell's work in his Ph.D. dissertation on extreme particularism stimulated me to rethink my own ideas on this topic, and Chapter 4 is the result. Two anonymous readers for the Cornell University Press provided useful comments. Roger Haydon of Cornell University Press was helpful and supportive. I thank all these people.

My greatest debt, once again, is to my wife, Sally Foster Wallace. Her advice and encouragement sustained me through this project.

NORMS AND PRACTICES

Introduction

Much of our lives is taken up with activity that can be described as participating in practices. We work at jobs, participate in family life, take part in civic activities and politics as citizens, and so on. Little reflection is necessary to realize that these practices we participate in are complex bodies of practical knowledge. The knowledge is know-how, what we take to be good ways or right ways to do certain things. The knowledge is thus normative. The practices are complexes of norms. Further, we acquire this knowledge from others. The practices in which we participate are social in character. The practices have a history. Generally they exist before we come on the scene, and we are inducted into them by others. We typically spend considerable time learning to be carpenters, lawyers, sheep farmers, researchers, and so on. We learn how properly to solve problems that arise in the practice, and sometimes as a result of our activity, the practice changes, if only marginally.

Generally, practices change only gradually. We can inquire into the history of a practice to discover how it has changed over time. Our lives, then, are for the most part made up of participating in practices that consist of complex bodies of norms. Learning the practice is both acquiring practical knowledge and acquiring norms. The knowledge acquired is based on experience—for the most part it depends on the experience of others that is then passed on to us.

On the basis of our own experience as practitioners, we add our bit to the practices we take part in. The practices we participate in are moving bodies of empirical knowledge. The norms that a practice comprises are items of empirical practical knowledge based upon discoveries of how to do things.

The foregoing seems obvious. Few will find anything to object to in it. Here, though, is the controversial part. Ethical norms are found among the norms that constitute the practices that make up so much of our lives, and these norms, too, are items of (presumptive) practical knowledge. Ethical norms are the result of the experience of many people over a long time. The norms are a part of their knowledge, such as it is, of how to live and work together and how to do a great many things. Ethical knowledge, too, is empirical knowledge. Ethical norms are subject to change, like any other social phenomena. As communities and their environments change, such norms need to change to deal with new problems.

English-speaking philosophers, over the last few centuries and up to the present, have defended several importantly different views of ethics. Most of these views are alike, however, in conceiving of moral norms as independent from the actual practices that make up the lives of human individuals and their communities. Indeed, whether these norms are conceived as the legislation of God or of Reason (God's Enlightenment avatar) or as somehow ingrained in the nature of things, there is nearly a consensus that these norms are independent from the contingencies and vicissitudes of historical practice.[1] It is assumed that since ethical norms are the standards for evaluating the practice of individuals and communities, they must in their existence and authority be independent from those practices. One result of this assumption is that ethical norms are

---

1. Among the exceptions are philosophers influenced by Hegel, including such American pragmatists as John Dewey and Richard Rorty. See Dewey, *Human Nature and Conduct* (1922); and Rorty, *Contingency, Irony, and Solidarity* (1989).

viewed as being fundamentally different in their origin, nature, and authority from the norms that practices comprise. It becomes a serious problem on this view to explain how ethical norms are even relevant to our lives. This is the source, I think, of many of the difficulties that are familiar to philosophers who study ethics.

This book offers a different conception of ethical norms and of the inquiry that studies them. Among the main claims of this book are the following. Ethical norms—standards by which actions are judged good or bad, right or wrong—are items of practical knowledge. These items of knowledge are components of practices that make up the lives of people. The practices and their component practical norms, including ethical norms, are the result of the experience over time of many people in dealing with the problems they encounter in living together and doing things. The practices are psychosocial phenomena, ways of living that people in a community share. The component norms of these practices, including ethical norms, are also psychosocial in nature. The norms as they exist in individuals consist in know-how, tendencies to act, generally tendencies that are complexly organized in groups. The activity that expresses these tendencies is typically participation in a practice such as medicine, family life, or democratic political life. The tendencies belong to individuals as psychological traits. Ethical norms, as components of practices, exist in a community in the same way that practices do. Actual practices change over time as their social-historical contexts change. As a result, ethical norms, too, change, develop, possibly improve. Since practical knowledge that constitutes practices is based upon the experience of people, it is a body of empirical knowledge.

A number of avenues are available for the study of norms that are components of practices. Individuals who have mastered a practice have a special perspective on many questions that pertain to the practice. If asked in a specific context, "What should be done here?" participants in the practice may consult their own know-how: "Here's what I would do." Such pronouncements are fallible and corrigible, but coming from competent practitioners, they have a certain authority.[2] We are typically in the position of participants with respect to ethical questions. Based upon our own practical knowledge, we can attempt to articulate what it is that we know. Caution is in order here. Any item of supposed practical knowledge may be mistaken. The mistake may be widely shared. In a particular case, a participant may be mistaken about what the norms of the practice actually indicate in that case. Even if we do know how to act in view of our having acquired the norm, we still may not be able to articulate that knowledge. With these caveats in mind, we can take seriously our understanding of ethical matters based upon our own knowhow. We ourselves are practitioners, and in studying ethics, we can, with appropriate caution, use our own know-how as practitioners, our knowledge of how things properly are done.

Since one's knowledge as a practitioner of what should be done in various situations is fallible, it is very helpful to discuss such matters with other practitioners, much as physicians do when they are puzzled by a difficult case. To understand the practices themselves and what their roles are in our lives, we can undertake an inquiry that might be called, for lack of a better word, interpretive.[3] Such inquiry is familiar to historians; it can be difficult. Possessing the knowledge that constitutes a practice is not sufficient for being able accurately to articulate that knowledge or to describe the practice generally, its strengths and weaknesses, and its relationships to other practices. Not every competent civil engineer can write a textbook about road building or discuss knowledgeably how public funds should be divided between maintenance of infrastructure,

2. Gary Ebbs discusses the "participant perspective" in practical knowledge in *Rule-Following and Realism* (1997), 247–52. He cites R. M. Hare's "Philosophical Discoveries" (1967), 206–17.

3. For discussions of this sort of inquiry concerning the roles and functions of practices, see J. D. Wallace, *Ethical Norms, Particular Cases* (1996), chapter 4, and R. Dworkin, *Law's Empire* (1986), chapters 1 and 2.

national defense, and health care. Aided by the knowledge available from the perspective of practitioners, practitioners can undertake to describe what they know. Historical inquiry into the development of practices and their norms is useful in understanding how they developed, what their successes and failures have been, and how they are related to one another in the life of a community. Historical examples are useful both in formulating and making explicit one's knowledge as a practitioner and for deepening one's understanding of the norms' origins, uses, and development.

Articulating the knowledge of practitioners, reflecting on the uses and functions of practices, and inquiring into the histories of practices are lines of inquiry that are generally combined in this book. Since ethical norms are items of empirical practical knowledge—know-how based on experience—this study of ethics is an empirical study. Historical examples are used extensively throughout this work, but so, too, are some fictional examples that are useful for making explicit to ourselves what we know as practitioners.

Chapter 1 develops the view of ethical norms as constituents of actual practices. One advantage of the idea that ethical norms are components of shared activities is to make ethics a phenomenon that is intrinsic to our very lives rather than an imposition somehow from outside. With the help of John Dewey's ideas, the chapter describes a way of understanding from this perspective practical reasoning and the role of ethics in reasoning. It defends in a preliminary way the view that existing practices can be effectively criticized by standards that are conceived as components of practices.

Frederick Will's distinction between the manifest and the latent content of norms is the topic of chapter 2. A particular norm may be formulated as a rule or instruction, and this will express the manifest content of the norm. Intelligently following the norm, however, often will consist in more than simply doing what its manifest content directs. Understanding a norm requires that one understand how the norm is followed in conjunction with other norms that a practice comprises; in Will's phrase, it requires an understanding of the "latent content" of norms. Since the latent content of norms generally resists complete formulation, the notion that norms provide rational guidance only through their manifest and explicit contents will leave out much that is crucial for intelligent activity in inquiry as well as law, politics, and ethics.

Social criticism—the criticism of practice—is the topic of chapter 3. The prejudice that searching criticism of actual practice is impossible without practice-independent norms is confronted by examples of just the sort of thing that is thought to be impossible. The argument that actual practice is too variable and conflicting to enable such criticism is examined and rejected. The search for practice-independent norms, based upon the assumption that such norms are necessary for social criticism, is therefore misguided. The discussion ranges over criticism of practice within a community, intercommunity social criticism, and the evaluation of practices of past communities.

Chapter 4 is a discussion of the roles, crucial for practical reasoning, of general and particular knowledge in intelligent action. Rule formalism conceives practical knowledge as embodied in general instructions or precepts that explicitly prescribe what to do in a range of situations. The view does not fit the facts, but when it is rejected, as it generally is these days, the alternatives seem most unattractive. The view that general rules and instructions are properly applied in hard cases by means of intuition in effect offers no account of how general precepts are properly applied. Extreme particularism, on the other hand, attempts to dispense with general practical knowledge altogether and attributes normative guidance to particular perceptions. By means of Will's conception of the latent content of norms, this chapter attempts to adjudicate among this triad of unsatisfactory accounts of the guidance of norms in hard cases. The aim is to preserve the place of general norms in practical knowledge without falling into the difficulties of rule formalism or intuitionism.

The tendencies that constitute the mastery of a practice are tendencies to act in accordance with norms, including ethical norms. Although the promptings of kindness, sympathy, and compassion can and sometimes do conflict with the tendencies to follow norms, the former virtues do belong to good character. Chapter 5 considers the relationship in individual character of certain tendencies to follow norms (virtues of justice) and virtues of benevolence that are focused on the welfare of individuals rather than on norms. The thesis is that benevolence is the perfection of people's appreciation of one another, a condition that supports the sociality necessary for complex practices and provides an appreciation of the point of those practices.

ONE   *Challenging the Paradigm in Ethics*

Two assumptions are deeply entrenched in Anglo-American philosophical ethics. The first assumption is that ethical norms have an origin, existence, and authority independent from actual historical social practice. The second assumption is that each individual could, in principle, gain knowledge of such norms independently of other individuals. Both assumptions have very long histories. We could call the first assumption the Platonic assumption about ethics and the second the Cartesian. There are at present competing, sharply contested accounts of what these timeless norms independent from practices are and how we know of them. We gain access to ethical norms that are independent from practice, according to some, by comparing our "intuitions" about what we should do, seeking interpersonal agreement in these intuitions, and rendering these consistent with one another. We gain access to ethical norms that are independent from practice, according to others, by working out what ideally rational persons would legislate in hypothetical situations. Behind these and other views about how we should act is the picture of an agency, reason, that speaks the same message to each of us, if only we will listen properly. This is the model that underlies the epistemological individualism of the Renaissance.

There is philosophy to the contrary in Hegel and certain philosophers influenced by Hegel, but the view that morality is fundamentally a social/historical phenomenon receives little attention now from Anglo-American philosophers. I describe and recommend a version of the view that ethical norms are social artifacts. So conceived, ethical norms are the precipitate of the discoveries and inventions over time of countless human beings, just as medicine or music are the result of the contributions of many. Our knowledge of such matters is based upon our experience; in that sense it is empirical. Like other kinds of empirical knowledge, the knowledge of how to act is corrigible and improvable. On this view, ethical norms *are* a kind of knowledge; they are items of *practical* knowledge. Such a norm is our understanding of how to do something. Ethical norms, together with other norms, constitute our shared knowledge, such as it is, of how to live with one another in communities as the kind of beings we are in the circumstances in which we live.

In the present intellectual and social climate, many things stand in the way of such a view's getting a serious hearing, by philosophers and others. If ethical norms are social artifacts, then these norms have a history; they sometimes undergo a development. The norms are changeable, improvable. According to this view, ethical knowledge develops in a community in response to the problems that its members and others have faced over time. This implies that communities, with different histories and circumstances, might have different ethical norms, different understandings of how properly to live with one another. It is also possible that the norms of a certain exotic community are better suited to that community's circumstances than our ethical norms would be. If norms are social artifacts, it is possible that our ethical norms are not as well suited to our circumstances as the norms of a certain exotic community are suited to their circumstances. These possibilities are deeply troubling to many people.

Here is another initial objection to the view that ethical norms are social artifacts: if ethical norms are themselves corrigible and improvable, by what standards can their correction properly be judged to be improvements? A central function of ethical norms is to serve as standards for assessing and criticizing actual practice. If *all* ethical norms are social artifacts that arise out of people's actual lives and practice, the norms are deeply implicated in their present practice. So conceived, such norms would lack the kind of independence of actual practice that would enable deep, searching criticism of the practices themselves. Our actual practices would, it seems, be the judges in their own cases, with no possibility of appeal.

Another objection, related to the preceding one, is that if the only norms available for the criticism of practice are components of actual practices, then too often we will be unable to resolve disagreements about practice. People in fact practice differently, and they have different and sometimes conflicting notions about what proper practice is in certain areas. To the extent that they disagree about how practices are properly pursued, and this difference is reflected in what they do, they are apt to disagree about any norms internal to those practices. Without norms independent from practice, there is no way to resolve such disagreements by rational means.

To assert that ethical norms are constituents of actual human practices will seem to many to denigrate morality. There is a powerful desire to set morality, like Platonic forms, apart from the vicissitudes of history and the danger of human error, imperfection, and corruption.

I set out the social artifact view of ethical norms and then, in this and later chapters, return to these and other objections to the view. This, however, can be said to the critics from the outset: on the social artifact conception, ethical norms *are* items of practical knowledge, know-how. They belong to the same genus, then, as other sorts of norms, such as the standards of right and wrong, better and worse, and practice in such matters as treating wounds, conducting international diplomacy, growing grain, and making bread. That norms of healing, politics, and so on change and develop, that these norms may be different at different times and in different communities, and that these norms are constituents of the very practices they govern does not necessarily undermine the authority, the usefulness, or the importance of such norms. There often is controversy about such practices and their norms. Still, we are frequently able, sometimes only over a long time and with difficulty, to resolve such controversies. So it is with ethical norms, too. It is apparent, also, that we have an abundance of ways of assessing and criticizing such norms—or so I argue.

I

The notions of a practice and a norm are central to this discussion. The conception of a practice derives from American pragmatists and from philosophers influenced by Wittgenstein. I am indebted to Alasdair MacIntyre's discussion of a practice in his book *After Virtue* (1984). The conception of a norm is adapted from the work of Frederick L. Will, in *Beyond Deduction: Ampliative Aspects of Philosophical Reflection* (1988) and from John Dewey's discussions of what he called, perhaps unfortunately, "habit" in his book *Human Nature and Conduct* (1922).

Basic to the social artifact conception of ethical norms is the conception of a practice. Practices are activities guided by a shared body of practical knowledge—knowledge of how to pursue the activity. Knowledge of how to do something is normative; it is knowledge of how to do it *properly*, knowledge of better rather than worse ways of doing things. So, often, the best way to exemplify a norm, say the right way to make a surgical incision, is by demonstrating the action. A practice *consists* in a structured body of norms. Norms are its constituents. Human life consists in participating in practices. Many practices require a complex body of cultivated, structured, shared practical knowledge. Think of expository writing, humanitarian relief work, building construction, democratic politics, and childrearing.

We are born into a life structured by a great number of practices; our education begins with induction into practices that are taught to us by other people. What is learned was and is shared, shaped by the cumulative discoveries of earlier practitioners of what conduces to achieving the purposes of the practices in a variety of circumstances. Practitioners then use their know-how. More or less unprecedented problems arise in individuals' practice, and when they are able to resolve such problems, they may share their experience with others. They may thereby extend the practice incrementally. In the process of extending the practice, it sometimes becomes evident that new purposes can be achieved by the practice. Thus, not only the norms of the practice are to a degree altered, but sometimes the practitioners' understanding of the purposes of the practice changes too. In *After Virtue*, Alasdair MacIntyre illustrates such a development with the example of the history of the practice of portrait painting in Europe from medieval times through the eighteenth century. Portrait painters first produced icons, generic faces with surrounding details to indicate whose face was represented. They eventually discovered that they could produce likenesses, representations of faces that looked like their subjects. Painters then strove to produce likenesses. It was later discovered that certain likenesses reveal the characters of their subjects, and portrait painters aimed at likenesses that expressed character. The norms of better and worse portrait painting, of course, changed as the purposes of portrait painters changed. This pattern recurs in other practices (MacIntyre 1984, 189).

Complex social practices require that practitioners aid and cooperate with one another. Among the norms—the items of practical knowledge—that contribute to the purposes of the practice, then, will be norms of honesty, forthrightness, mutual aid, trustworthiness, fairness, respect, and fellowship among practitioners. Of course, these norms are ones we recognize as ethical norms. Among the norms of practices, then, will be ethical norms.

Practices exist within larger communities. Often, the purposes of the practices, their fruits, are socially important to the community. In communities, many practices are pursued together in close proximity to one another. It is not surprising, then, to find that among the norms that constitute particular practices are norms that guide practitioners in conducting their activity in harmony with other practices. A particular practice, then, will reflect in its norms the particular circumstances in which it is practiced, including its social context.

These matters are extremely complicated in an actual community. The *Republic* of Plato, with its transparency and simplicity, provides a useful and familiar model for understanding some important interconnections among a community, its practices, and its members. Plato said, "A *polis* [community] comes to be because none of us is self-sufficient, but we all need many things" (1992, 44 [369b]). He explained this in the following way. A human being's needs and desires generally are far more extensive than the individual's abilities to fulfill them. Different individuals, however, have different skills and aptitudes, so in a large enough group of people, the various abilities can be found for meeting a considerable number of any individual's concerns. Not only does the division of labor in a community promise that more rather than fewer of people's needs and interests will be fulfilled through the efforts of others, but it also provides the social circumstances for groups of people with similar aptitudes to share practical knowledge and cultivate together their productive activity. Generally, each specialized group, each "guild," so to speak, requires the support of other subgroups to provide for its members' needs and interests. Thus we have community.

The social arrangement Plato described makes it possible for people to specialize by devoting themselves to mastering practices that comprise elaborate bodies of cultivated, shared practical knowledge. It provides the circumstances necessary for individuals' acquiring and manifesting such practical knowledge. Plato, of course, thought that norms are radically independent from practices—he made the Platonic assumption—so I am borrowing certain of his social ideas to make very un-Platonic points about norms. When you or I in a community act in ways that manifest complex practical knowledge—perhaps we conduct inquiry, teach, treat illnesses, or make music—we are participating in social practices. These practices are in fact social artifacts, social transmits, shared bodies of moving, changing practical knowledge about what is valuable in a certain domain and how these valuable things are properly fostered and protected. Such a practice is the result of the practical experience of many people over time; the practical knowledge is in this sense derived from experience. The practice itself is a complex norm. It is, in Frederick L. Will's words, a "composition of norms" (1988, 147–48). Different groups of people in a single community cultivate different practices, and the resulting division of labor generally contributes to fulfilling the myriad needs and interests of the community at large and its members. So a practice needs a community.

Plato's model of a community fits many communities well, including our own. Although the model focuses only on the practices that constitute work in a system of division of labor, it indicates how thoroughly interconnected and complexly interrelated are norms, practices, and communities. Some norms of a practice will indicate how practitioners should act in order to foster attainment of the purposes of the practice. Because a practice will be a group undertaking, some of its constituent norms will concern how practitioners should act toward one another to foster the attainment of their collective purposes. Norms pertaining to cooperation, trust, and mutual aid will be prominent among the norms of a practice. Equally important in such practices are harmonizing and coordinating the pursuit of each practice with *other* practices and activities that are carried on in the same community. The various practices must be pursued simultaneously in proximity to one another. Plato teaches us that this is not an accident. It is important that the various activities interfere with one another as little as possible. So, for example, dumping waste in lakes and rivers might be the most efficient means of disposal for some manufacturers, but such dumping disrupts other areas of life in the community. Such polluting is bad practice in manufacturing. If the practices in a community reinforce one another, so much the better. Norms that contribute to the harmony of one practice with other practices and with the larger life of the community will be among the norms of the more important practices. To the extent that a practice cannot be harmonized with other practices in a community it is a bad practice. Thus, no matter how effectively the members of the guild of thieves realize their purposes, their practice is a bad one.

A practice requires a degree of consensus among practitioners and others about the purposes of the activities and how those purposes are best achieved. This agreement is expressed in the way that people are taught the practice, the similarities in the ways that such individuals act, and in their criticisms of their own and others' practice. At the same time, practices are typically surrounded by controversy. Think of law, inquiry, art, government, education, marriage, and so on. Almost anything about a sophisticated practice, it seems, can be contested. Such controversies may seem, as Michael Walzer noted in *Just and Unjust Wars,* "painful, sustained, exasperating, and endless," but they are symptomatic of the fact that practitioners have and exercise a critical attitude that is necessary for the growth of a practice and its adaptation to changing social and physical circumstances (1977, 11). If a practice is to be vital, it must be possible for participants to disagree; if the practice is to be viable, it must be possible for them to agree. The result, if the practice flourishes, is a moving, changing consensus, often accompanied by considerable noise and some confusion.

II

Complex social practices consisting of cultivated bodies of practical knowledge exist only when individuals actually have the knowledge and act upon it. Similarly, the norms that a practice comprises exist only when individuals understand and act upon them. A practice, regarded as practical knowledge in individuals, is a complex instance of what John Dewey called a "habit." Here is Dewey's definition.

> The word habit may seem twisted somewhat from its customary use...But we need a word to express that kind of human activity which is influenced by prior activity and in that sense acquired; which contains within itself a certain ordering or systematization of minor elements of action; which is projective, dynamic in quality, ready for overt manifestation; and which is operative in some sub-dued subordinate form even when not obviously dominating activity. (Dewey 1922, 31)

A practice, regarded as a complex norm, is a social phenomenon, a shared body of practical knowledge in a community. It is, at the same time, a psychological phenomenon, a complex shared habit of individuals in Dewey's terminology, a shared, structured set of skills, know-how, understandings, tendencies of thought and action, and appreciations. So, what an individual learns in a school of law or a music conservatory is a complex habit, in Dewey's sense of the term. An individual expresses this "habit" by participating in the practice and in other ways. A norm, as Frederick Will put it in *Pragmatism and Realism*, is a "sociopsychological entity" (1997, 166).

Because particular practices are more or less adapted to other practices of the community, each practice will to a degree reflect those other practices and the circumstances and history of the community. Contemporary medicine provides a useful example. It changes very rapidly, and there is a constant struggle to adjust the norms of its practice to one another and to the changing social and scientific context. Its practice is not only attuned to the effective production of certain important results pertaining to health, but it also is practiced in ways that take account of the larger social context. Medicine is shaped in part by this context, and it has a reciprocal effect on its social environment. We are currently keenly aware of the extent to which medicine is practiced in ways that comport with and in ways that conflict with economic, political, educational, and religious matters.

Communities organized in accordance with a principle of division of labor will comprise more or less harmonized cultivated practices that serve their members' purposes more or less effectively. Because of continually changing circumstances, any harmonization, any successful adjustment of practices to one another, is temporary; the need for readjustment is never-ending. Members of a community will participate in a variety of other practices in addition to the activity that falls to them by a division of labor. Friendships, families, marketplaces, political parties, religions, and other associations must be harmonized within the life of the community and within the lives of individual members. The more resourceful individuals and groups are, when confronted with conflicts and dislocations that result from such changes, the better. Of course, the more we know of other communities and their practices, the larger our potential resources for altering our own practices. Think of China's attempts to integrate into their lives first Marxist ideas and then a free market economy.

When an individual masters a particular practice and participates in it effectively, what the individual will have acquired is a complex Deweyan habit of acting in accordance with a body of norms that are shaped in part by the purposes of the practice and in part by the necessity of harmonizing the practice with the other practices of the community. The individual's psychical structure is the adjustment in the individual of myriad Deweyan habits, all, as Dewey says, "projective, dynamic in quality, ready for overt manifestation."

In this way, a person's habits tend to operate even when they are not obviously dominating present activity. A geologist, even when on vacation, will notice and react to things that the rest of us miss. The less harmoniously habits are adjusted to one another within the individual psyche, the more apt the person is to be ineffective, fumbling, hesitating, inconsistent, or erratic in action. The individual's psychical structure, Dewey said, is the person's character (1922, 29–30).

A community, then, as Plato discovered, is a good model for the human psyche. An individual's problems will reflect to a considerable degree the community's continuing efforts to adapt and harmonize important activities of its members. An individual attempts to be at once a friend, colleague, worker, family member, citizen, and so on. This effort requires the individual to follow simultaneously a great many norms. In view of the complexity of human life and the variety of circumstances that people encounter, there are constant conflicts among the demands of these norms. Novel situations bring about unprecedented conflicts. Much of an individual's intellectual and moral effort in the practical sphere is directed at resolving such conflicts by harmonizing the many norms of a single practice and the norms of other practices that constitute the social context. The problems of an entire community and the problems of its individual members will not be identical, like mirror images, but they will substantially reflect one another in their content as well as their form.

III

Practical reasoning, including reasoning involving moral considerations, is a form of problem solving. In its more interesting and challenging instances, it is more than the routine application of pre-existing problem-solving procedures to a current problem. Practical problems that challenge us typically present novel juxtapositions of norms in unprecedented conflicts. Past experience with solving more or less similar problems is an indispensable resource in dealing with novel problems, but this resource may be altered and adapted in applying it to the new problem. Practical reasoning at its best is improvisational and creative. The solution to a novel problem may alter one or more of the conflicting norms in order to make an activity more effective or to harmonize the norm with other norms. Such an alteration changes the practice itself. It may result in the creation of a new norm. If the problem involves ethical norms in the conflict, a solution may change one or more of the ethical norms. An alteration of a moral norm *might* involve a betrayal of the very point of the moral consideration so altered, but it need not. It may instead be an alteration that enables individuals to follow all the conflicting norms at once to achieve something like their original purpose, in a way that is faithful to an appreciable extent to what is at stake in all the competing norms. An understanding of the conflicting norms, the norms' roles in practices, and what the practices mean in people's lives are the guides to good choices in such problems.

This very general characterization of practical problem solving will seem vague, but the generality is commensurate with the variety of the phenomenon characterized. Examples of actual problem solving are useful in clarifying this account, but good examples tend to be complicated. What follows are some examples of extended deliberations of entire communities. In seventeenth-century Europe, the state's traditional role as protector of an official religious orthodoxy conflicted with the acceptance in some quarters of the developing idea that religion is a private matter. In the midst of the religious wars of the time and cruel persecutions, the idea gained currency that religious heterodoxy per se is not a threat to the welfare of the community. Long ago, people had believed that heterodoxy caused great calamities such as famine, floods, and plagues. Gradually, over the centuries this belief was given up, but the idea persisted that religious heterodoxy is somehow dangerous to a community, despite the fact that people no longer believed that it was a cause of specific social calamities. The idea thus persisted long after it had lost its rationale. European people gradually became aware of a state of affairs that had existed for centuries—that the enforcement of religious orthodoxy could no longer be defended as a part of the state's function of protecting the public safety. A norm of civic toleration of religious diversity arose from an altered understanding of the roles of state and religion. These developments were not guided by a pre-existing norm of freedom of religion; rather the norm was created by the developments themselves. As Dewey noted in *The Public and Its Problems*, both religion and the state's function as protector of the public weal came to be understood differently, in a way that enabled them to exist more compatibly, and norms of freedom of religion emerged as the result of this harmonization (1927, 266–67).

The practice of nonviolent civil disobedience of the law in democracies developed as a way of harmonizing to a degree the rule of law with the duty to oppose injustices when the majority refuses to redress the injustices. Minorities, apparently faced with a stark choice between acquiescing in injustice or engaging in violent revolution, could in some circumstances oppose injustices effectively while at the same time expressing their allegiance to law and majority rule by acting nonviolently and accepting the legal penalties for their disobedience. Gandhi's home-rule campaign in India in 1920 and the civil rights movement in the United States in the 1960s are examples of such activities (Rawls 1971, 1999, 319–23, 326–31).

The gradual abandonment in Europe in the fifteenth and sixteenth centuries of the idea that lending money at interest is a form of extortionate theft and the emergence of the standard of a fair rate of interest tended to harmonize important norms of property and entitlement with the demands for capital in a developing investment economy. In earlier subsistence economies, loans tended to be a form of charity to a neighbor in need. The lender had a right to ask for the eventual return of the principal but had no legitimate claim to anything in addition to the principal. A borrower would agree to return eventually more than the principal only out of desperation. Lenders who demanded interest on loans thus tended to be viewed as extortionists of opportunity. When investment became more common, and money became a commodity, it was possible for lenders to claim that they were entitled to interest on a loan proportional to the profit they might make investing the money elsewhere. In this case, as Albert Jonsen and Stephen Toulmin mention in *The Abuse of Casuistry*, historical change resulted in the abandonment of the idea that lending at interest is theft and the adoption of the idea of a fair rate of interest on a loan (1988, 181–94).

John Dewey described the proper aim of deliberation as "unifying, harmonizing, different competing tendencies." "[Intelligent choice] may release an activity in which all are fulfilled, not indeed, in their original form, but in a 'sublimated' fashion, that is in a way which modifies the original direction of each by reducing it to a component along with others in an action of transformed quality" (Dewey 1922, 135).

Dewey's account holds for the deliberations, the practical reasoning, of individuals as individuals and for the sometimes extended deliberations of groups, of communities. The problems people confront in their actions typically take the form, How am I (or how are we) to be faithful to this norm while at the same time continuing to observe effectively the many other norms that pertain to what I am now doing (or what we are now doing)? A physician struggles to respond to reasonable requirements to reduce the costs of medical care while providing patients with the best care possible. An engineer must complete projects in a timely way while maintaining a high standard of safety. People with time-consuming jobs attempt to fulfill family responsibilities. The desired solution in all such cases, of course, would enable us to continue to achieve the purposes of the practices involved, though purposes may be altered in the process, too. It is not enough that our norms simply be coherent with one another.

In Dewey's words, the good we seek in deliberation "is never twice alike. It never copies itself. It is new every morning, fresh every evening. It is unique in its every presentation. For it marks the resolution of a distinctive complication of competing habits and impulses which can never repeat itself" (1922, 146).

Dewey's account offers an important alternative to a more linear conception of deliberation, practical reasoning, that has been influential at least since Aristotle. On the linear view, deliberation begins with a clearly conceived end or result that the agent desires. Deliberating, then, consists in a search for effective means for realizing that end. It makes a considerable difference whether one conceives of practical reasoning as harmonizing conflicting considerations or as seeking a means to a preconceived, pre-existing end. For one thing, on the Deweyan view, deliberation frequently begins with a conflict of norms and "impulses." One attains a relatively clear and concrete conception of the aimed-at result only when the deliberation is successfully completed and the problem solved. The "distinctive complication" of practical considerations will be resolved successfully by altering one or more of the considerations so that all can be more or less fulfilled simultaneously. Of course, nothing guarantees success in such an undertaking.

The Aristotelian account of deliberation, taken to cover all deliberations, implies that we are equipped at the outset with clearly and concretely articulated purposes, goals, or ends that will provide us with our starting point for deliberation. Something like this is true in certain deliberations. In this way, a householder figures out how to deal with a clogged drain. A golfer's end of getting the ball in the hole in as few strokes as possible is relatively clear and fixed ahead of time. In many challenging practical circumstances, however, we are not guided at the outset by a concrete conception of the outcome we want. We are in the position of certain modern young people who are deciding what to do with their lives. In a certain circumstance, to change the example, someone is determined to give all concerned their due, to be fair to everyone. But what is that, in this particular situation? Here, what it is to be fair in this situation needs to be determined, and this can be done only by deliberating. One does not begin with a clear conception of what is fair in the circumstances. Besides failing to describe accurately what in fact takes place in many actual deliberations, the Aristotelian view of deliberation leads to vexed—I believe, insoluble—problems about what these fixed purposes are and where they come from.

Following the ancient Greeks, we think of a "craft," including professions, as aiming at a particular clearly defined purpose or good. So health, for example, is the aim of medicine. This truism supports the misconception that physicians in their clinical decisions have a purpose that is clearly conceived ahead of time, health, that is their goal with particular patients. Their art, according to the misconception, consists in finding the means with patients of attaining this clearly conceived end. In fact, though, clinical problems generally involve a complex of difficulties, multiple things wrong with the patient, and the clinician's task is to find courses of treatment that will ameliorate some of these problems without causing (too many) other ones, and that will fit the patient's particular way of living. What this desired result is in concrete terms is not clear ahead of time. In these cases, too, the good achieved is unique to the situation and is discovered and articulated only as a result of the deliberations. Health, the good that is the end of medicine, is in fact not the clearly articulated goal that is the aim of every clinical medical decision.

Dewey generalized this point.

We cannot seek or attain health, wealth, learning, justice, or kindness in general. Action is always specific, concrete, individualized, unique. And consequently judgments as to acts to be performed must be similarly specific....How to live healthily or justly is a matter which differs with every person. It varies with his past experience, his opportunities, his temperamental and acquired weaknesses and abilities. Not man in general but a particular man suffering from some particular disability aims to live healthily, and consequently health cannot mean for him exactly what it means for any other mortal. Healthy living is not something to be attained by itself apart from other ways of living. (Dewey 1920, 175)

Dewey does not deny that general goods play a role in practical reasoning.

The general notions of health, disease, justice, artistic culture are important. Not, however, because this or that case may be brought exhaustively under a single head and its specific traits shut out, but because generalized science provides a man as physician and artist and citizen, with questions to ask, investigations to make, and enables him to understand the meaning of what he sees. (1920, 176)

On the Aristotelian linear account of practical reasoning, two conditions must be satisfied in any choice for it to be a right choice. First, the act chosen must be an effective means to the proposed goal, and, second, the proposed goal must itself be good. One can sometimes show that the goal is good because it, in turn, is conducive to a further purpose that is good, but this process cannot go on ad infinitum. If any choice is justified, then on the Aristotelian view there must be at least one good that is good for its own sake to which every right choice in the end conduces. The notion that every right choice is justified by its conducing to some final good or goods faces the difficulty of finding plausible candidates for the role of the final good or goods. One cannot explain why a final good is good—it just is. Unsatisfying appeals to "self-evidence" are tempting here. (See, for example, Finnis 1980, 64–69.) Further, the more specific one makes the description of the final goods, the more difficult it will be to establish that *every* right choice will advance just *these* goals.

If the final good(s) are characterized in very general terms, however, it will not be plausible to claim that the characterization is specific enough to determine choices in complex situations. It is plausible (perhaps) to say that good choices will be those that conduce to "living well as a human being," but without a more specific description of what living well is, it will be hard to know what choices conduce to it. Living well takes many forms. If we suppose that there is more than one final good, what will we do when two or more of these goods conflict in a particular case? How will we choose between them? These and other difficulties with the linear conception of practical reasoning are discussed in more detail in James D. Wallace, *Moral Relevance and Moral Conflict* (1988), chapter 4.

Our environment changes continually, and we must constantly adapt our practices to unforeseen developments. Ethical norms must change if we are to respond effectively to change. It is equally important, however, that the norms in other respects remain the same. The norms embody what knowledge we have of how to deal with problems already encountered, and this is a precious resource that we must conserve. Our attitude toward this knowledge must be at once reformist and conservative. It is crucial, of course, that the right things be changed and the right things be conserved.

In general, one should not lie. To do so generally violates important norms of communication and cooperation. Lying tends to create havoc in human affairs. The web we thereby weave can be very tangled indeed. Since human activities and practices require both communication and cooperation, a norm of truthfulness is generally found in all areas of life and, with local variations, across cultures. In every practice, though, a norm of truthfulness is encountered by practitioners together with a host of other norms, all of which need to be observed if the practice is to be done properly. The norm of truthfulness and these other norms will, through previous practice, have been to a degree adapted and adjusted to one another. One desideratum in adapting a norm of truthfulness in a practice is that communication and trust be preserved as far as possible, that the results of the havoc-creating tendency of lying and deception be forestalled. The norm of truthfulness, so adapted, may, as a result, differ somewhat from practice to practice. As practices develop and change, new adaptations and adjustments of a norm of truthfulness emerge. Think of family life, advocacy, the game of poker, psychotherapy, international diplomacy, and so on, and consider the norm of truthfulness that is a constituent of each. The norm of truthfulness cannot be "absolute"—tell the truth no matter what—because we encounter it together with other norms which from time to time conflict with truthfulness. Some of these norms are of an importance commensurate with the importance of the norm of truthfulness. The requirement of truthfulness cannot be unchanging because the physical and social world changes, practices change, and the norm, together with other norms, must offer guidance for living in such a world. The exceptions and adjustments cannot all be built into the norm ahead of time, because it is impossible to predict the novel problems a changing world will present. Practical knowledge—and, therefore, ethical knowledge—is necessarily open, unfinished.

IV

According to the philosopher T. M. Scanlon in "Contractualism and Utilitarianism," a satisfactory account of ethics "must make it understandable why moral reasons are ones that people can take seriously, and why they strike those who are moved by them as reasons of a special stringency and inescapability" (1982, 106). The view of ethical norms as social artifacts, I believe, satisfies these requirements. Those who take part simultaneously in many practices, and that is all of us, cannot escape the dominion of a variety of ethical norms. Those who care about the activities that constitute their lives, by that very fact care about acting in accordance with the activities' norms. Ethical norms that are crucial components of our practices will have an importance commensurate with the importance of those practices. What is distinctive about the form of life that is characteristic of human beings is that it consists in taking part in practices. These practices give our lives meaning. When such norms are conceived as social artifacts, it is apparent that the authority that they have derives from our recognition of their importance in our practices, the substance of our lives. The authority of moral standards, Dewey said, "is that of life" (1922, 57).

Philosophers who are sympathetic to deontological accounts of ethics may think that the view I recommend offers the wrong sort of reasons for following ethical norms. At best, they may object, the view would have us doing the right things for ignoble reasons, as Immanuel Kant's notorious shopkeeper treated customers honestly because a reputation for cheating is bad for business. Morality, it is sometimes said, demands that we observe its norms for their own sake and not because of the results of following the norms. The view of ethical norms as social artifacts construes these norms, in effect, as intellectual instruments, tools we employ for achieving the purposes of our practices in a community. This is the point of observing ethical norms on the view of ethical norms as social artifacts. Observing ethical norms in this spirit, from the deontological perspective, would not be observing the norms for *moral* reasons.

In fact, in particular circumstances, there is usually a variety of reasons for following a pertinent moral norm, and I doubt that the reasons divide easily into moral and nonmoral. For one thing, the different reasons tend to be interrelated. A scientific researcher, for example, may need immediate experimental results of a certain sort in order to get a grant renewed or to get tenure. Unfortunately, the results are not forthcoming, so the researcher makes up results and publishes them. There are many reasons why it is wrong to perpetrate such a scientific fraud. One who fakes scientific results is doing very bad science. An investigator who does this, moreover, is betraying science, subverting the practice of scientific inquiry. The fraud betrays colleagues' trust, and if other scientists are deceived, their own work may be adversely affected. Scientific fraud poisons the well of the scientific community. It tends to affect adversely everyone who has a stake in the effectiveness of scientific inquiry, and this includes more or less everyone.

These are *some* of the reasons why scientists should be scrupulously honest in reporting the results of their work. The norm applies to every inquirer; there is no escaping it. It is compelling just because so much depends upon its careful observance. A scientist who is affected by none of these considerations would be a peculiar scientist indeed. Of course, there are scientists who perpetrate scientific frauds. A scientist who publishes fraudulent results, though, saying, "just this once," is a person who is conflicted.

Have I overlooked a special distinctive *moral* reason for following a norm of truthfulness in science? Consider this: some people are committed to honesty and integrity quite generally, and for this reason they would not violate a trust. To do so would be for them a matter for considerable shame and regret, quite independently of the results that might flow from such a breach of integrity. Such people could be relied upon quite generally to follow norms of truthfulness in science and elsewhere. Here is a candidate for a *special* moral motive.

What, though, gives such a commitment to honesty its point? What makes it desirable and admirable? One answer is that practices are social, and truthfulness is of great importance in maintaining the mutual trust necessary for social practices to flourish and people to flourish in those practices. For these among other reasons, integrity, honesty, is valuable, and honest people are admirable.

Integrity is not the only value to which scientists might be committed in a way that quite generally motivates them to follow moral norms of truthfulness. Some scientists are committed to excellence in their practice—doing science in the right way and doing it well. For them, to do bad science in a particular circumstance would occasion considerable shame and regret, whatever the actual results of their poor performance. They, too, are reliably motivated to observe scrupulously the norms of good scientific practice, including the norm of truthfulness and other ethical norms the practice comprises. One can value and admire excellence in a particular practice for its own sake in much the same way that one can value honesty. One can value and admire excellence in practice generally. The reason why such commitments—to honesty and to excellence—are valuable, however, is that they are commitments to norms that are essential components of practices, including practices that are of the first importance.

In *What We Owe to Each Other*, T. M. Scanlon offers a complex account of moral reasons from a contractualist point of view that offers a way of sorting the many reasons scientists have for being truthful about their work (1998, 147–77). The reason why it is morally wrong to perpetrate a scientific fraud, on Scanlon's view, is that the action "would be disallowed by any set of principles for the general regulation of behavior that no one could reasonably reject as a basis for informed, unforced general agreement" (1998, 153). Scanlon explains why this is a reason by pointing out that living together on reasonable, mutually agreeable terms is particularly desirable and valuable. When an action is wrong for this sort of reason, there is a moral reason not to do the action. The central part of morality, according to Scanlon, is to be found in duties to other people, what people owe to one another according to principles that they could not reasonably reject (1998, 154). So on Scanlon's view, honesty is valuable and desirable because of its centrality to living with other people on reasonable, mutually agreeable terms. It is this relationship to "an ideal of relations to others" that makes honesty a moral reason (155). That scientific fraud is bad science is a reason for honesty in science, but it is not on Scanlon's account a moral reason.

Or so it appears initially: Scanlon allows that there is a wider understanding of the moral according to which acting out of loyalty to a friend or from a commitment to practicing well might qualify as acting from a moral reason (1998, 166–67, 172–73). He does think, however, that there is something particularly compelling about reasons that flow from "the positive value of living with others on terms they could not reasonably reject" (1998, 162). Our attitude toward people who are not concerned with this sort of unity with their fellows is different from our attitude toward people who are not concerned with excellence in an important practice (1998, 159). The former exhibit an attitude toward *us* that is particularly troubling.

For many people, the fact that an act is dishonest is sufficient reason not to do it. Scanlon, however, supplies an illuminating explanation of why this is a reason—it flows from a particularly desirable and valuable relationship with other people that involves living together on reasonable, mutually agreeable terms. This explanation provides a higher-order reason not to act dishonestly. Nothing compels us, however, to accept this as a bedrock explanation of this reason. This relationship of mutuality is itself important, desirable, and valuable because it has a central place in social practices. It is a sine qua non condition for the practices that make up our lives. Following moral norms in this spirit of mutuality exemplifies acting from one sort of moral reason. It is also true, however, that just as a concern with excellence is a condition for scientific inquiry, Scanlon's relationship among people is crucial for any practice.

There are different sorts of reasons for observing ethical norms that in the usual course of things reliably motivate people to observe the norms. I see no reason not to call all of these moral reasons. One who is disposed to follow a norm for any of these reasons is admirable. Such dispositions are important and valuable. To explain why any of these types of personality is admirable, valuable, and important, we can point to the role that people so motivated play in their practices and communities.

V

I cannot help thinking that those who believe that moral norms are depreciated by viewing them as components of actual practices do not have a proper appreciation of practices. Actual practices have faults, and some of these faults are painfully apparent. Still, practices are often extraordinary gifts of the past to us. Practices make us; they form us. They make possible our lives and our better moments. Dewey rose to heights of eloquence in his appreciation of human practices.

> The eternal dignity of labor and art lies in their effecting that permanent reshaping of environment which is the substantial foundation of future security and progress. Individuals flourish and wither away like the grass of the fields. But the fruits of their work endure and make possible the development of further activities having fuller significance. It is of grace not of ourselves that we lead civilized lives. There is sound sense in the old pagan notion that gratitude is the root of all virtue. Loyalty to whatever in the established environment makes a life of excellence possible is the beginning of all progress. The best we can accomplish for posterity is to transmit unimpaired and with some increment of meaning the environment that makes it possible to maintain the habits of decent and refined life. Our individual habits are links in forming the endless chain of humanity. Their significance depends upon the environment inherited from our forerunners, and it is enhanced as we foresee the fruits of our labors in the world in which our successors live. (Dewey 1922, 19)

TWO   *The Spirit of the Enterprise*

Frederick L. Will's views about the phenomena that he calls the governance of norms of thought and action grew out of his work on skepticism, truth, and the problem of induction. The professional activities of scientists, mathematicians, and philosophers—theoreticians—are the focus of his attention as he seeks to provide a basis for a critical understanding of their activities. The account he offers in his later work of how theorists properly proceed in cultivating and expanding an understanding of various phenomena, however, is an application of a more general conception of what it is for any human activity to proceed rightly, intelligently, appropriately. So, Will's description of how norms govern activity embraces—in addition to inquiry and theorizing—politics, law, ethics, art, professions, crafts, and the activities of everyday living. One consequence of this way of conceiving matters is that many of the problems that we presently distribute among the subdisciplines of philosophy for separate consideration turn out on Will's view to be amenable to strikingly similar treatment. Issues in law, politics, and ethics are used to shed light on issues in the philosophy of science. Philosophy, practiced as Will does, becomes once again a unified subject. The understanding of one area of life is used to illuminate other areas in a synthesis reminiscent of Plato's *Republic* in its comprehensiveness. The discussion that follows focuses on the very considerable illumination that Will's approach brings to issues in moral, social, and political philosophy.

I

An outstanding feature of Will's account of the governance of norms is connected with his distinction between the manifest and the latent aspects of a norm. A "norm" here can be understood as a learned activity that is taken to be an appropriate way to proceed in a certain domain (Will 1988, 30–31). In its manifest aspect, the norm is a guide in the sense of an instruction, a "template" for action: as the unit comes down the assembly line, I am instructed to wire a red and green striped resistor across the two terminals that protrude from it. This norm can be taken as defining my rather simple job, although the instruction does suppose that I know how to do such things as identifying resistors, sorting them by color, and connecting a resistor to two terminals. We can think of learned ways of identifying resistors, sorting them by color, wiring a resistor to a terminal, and so on, as component norms that, properly related one to another, make up the norm that governs my job. My job is simply one activity which, together with many other such activities, constitutes the activity, the enterprise of producing some product. The larger enterprise can be thought of as comprising a structured set of norms. The enterprise of making this product is itself a component of ever larger structures of economic and productive activities, which are in turn components of the life of an entire community.

Even the relatively simple matters involved in my assembly-line job exhibit considerable complexity. In its manifest aspect, my job norm directs me to do the same operation over and over. Its content can be captured in a brief description that can be used as an instruction, an order, a reminder, or the like. The manifest aspect is sufficient for the routine case—here comes another unit, I turn it so that the terminals are accessible, I pick up a red and green striped resistor, and so on. One day, though, I look for a red and green striped resistor and there aren't any there—and here comes another unit. My job norm does not cover this contingency. I am paralyzed. Presumably, somebody knows what to do when this happens—more red and green striped resistors need to be obtained, but how is this done, and what happens to the assembly line in the meanwhile? Should I let the units go by without the resistor installed? Should the assembly line be stopped? Suppose someone knows about the relationship of volts, amperes, and ohms, and tells me that three yellow and brown striped resistors are the equivalent of one red and green striped one. Should I wire three yellow and brown striped resistors across the two terminals of each unit and send it on down the line? The answer to this question depends on many things. Can the unit with three resistors across the terminals fit with the other components farther down the line when the final product is assembled? Is there room for the unit so configured in the box that houses the final product? Are the yellow and brown striped resistors appreciably more expensive than the red and green ones? Will there be additional expense in adapting other components to the unit with three resistors? Will such expenses matter?

Probably, running out of a part needed on a particular assembly line is sufficiently common so that there will be well-worked-out procedures to cope with such an occurrence. In Will's terminology, my job norm is then supplemented with an additional norm that explicitly covers this contingency in its manifest aspect. In other words, I have an instruction that tells me what to do if I run out of red and green resistors. Unprecedented occurrences for which I have no instruction are bound to occur, however, even on an assembly line. This is a hard fact about the human predicament that is of the greatest importance. I am imagining that on my job, running out of a certain kind of resistor is unprecedented, so that there exists no norm that indicates explicitly—that is, in its manifest content—what should be done. There are many things one might consider in the absence of an explicit direction covering such a contingency. Here, we encounter what Will calls, in "The Philosophic Governance of Norms," the latent aspect of norms. Norms are "components of larger complexes of human life and practice" (Will 1997, 165). "They are typically, and always at least to some degree, in dynamic relation with other features of life, including other norms, in consequence of which they are liable to alteration both in respect to the conditions under which they are properly applied and to the character of the responses that are proper to their application.... Norms are always in some degree open, rather than closed with respect to their manifest aspects" (1997, 166. Compare Will 1988, 147–52).

The job norm that constitutes my task at the assembly line indicates an activity that is part of an entire process of creation of a final product. The activity is economic—I and many others are engaged in earning a living. The process is productive; its purpose is to provide something that answers to some desire or need of people. These activities, too, will be constituted by a complex of norms. The way to work out what I should do when the manifest direction of my job's norm fails is by reference to the "larger complexes of human life and practice." Consider the entire productive and economic activity of which my job is a part. Certain things I might do when I run out of red and green resistors on the line will minimize the disruption of the larger enterprise, and to that extent these responses will be preferable. If I understand the larger activity of which my job is a part, I will be able to identify the less disruptive responses. I may even be able to find a response that will actually advance the larger enterprise in some respect, and this would be even better. By hypothesis, no existing norm in the complex available to guide the entire economic and productive process explicitly indicates or directs my proper course of action when I run out of red and green resistors. I am not necessarily bereft of any guidance whatsoever. The collection of norms that constitute the larger undertaking can intimate how one in my predicament should proceed.

I may be able to modify my job's norm in the light of the body of norms defining the larger activity in which I am taking part—by appealing to the latent aspect of the complex of norms that constitute the larger activity.

The latent aspect of norms that guides one in working out what to do when some unprecedented difficulty arises with one's assembly-line job is not something that belongs to the job norm as an isolated thing. It is this norm, together with the enterprise of which it is a part, with all its normative components, that guides one in working out the reasonable thing to do with an unprecedented difficulty. In other words, the job norm has a latent content in virtue of its place in and relationship to a complex body of norms.

Problems analogous to running out of the proper resistor on the assembly line arise for inquirers. In the early seventeenth century, William Harvey measured the quantity of blood that left the human heart with every contraction and estimated that in one hour, a quantity of blood leaves the heart whose weight exceeds the weight of a human being. For us now, this result confirms the established fact that the blood circulates in the body, returning continuously to the heart that functions as a pump. For an anatomist in Harvey's time, his result was deeply puzzling. Galen taught that blood ebbed and flowed in two independent systems, the veins and the arteries. The system of blood vessels in the human body did not appear to form a loop—there was no apparent way for the blood that left the heart to be channeled back to it. On the assumption that the blood does not circulate, however, there is no way to account for the origin of the enormous quantity of blood that leaves the heart on Harvey's showing and no way to explain what eventually becomes of it. The assumption that the blood circulates, on the other hand, requires that there be a circuit of vessels, but no such thing was found in dissections.

What supported Harvey in his conclusion that the blood must circulate was, of course, connected with the entire state of the knowledge of physiology at the moment of his discovery. The "smaller circulation" from the right side of the heart to the lungs and back to the left side of the heart had been described. Harvey's teacher, Fabricius, discovered in veins valves that impede the flow of blood away from the heart. Of very great influence, however, was the importance of mechanical things to the people of Harvey's time. Clocks, telescopes, artillery, and other machines, including pumps, were effecting a social and intellectual revolution. The operation of mechanical things was intelligible. Important people were mechanically minded, and the discovery that the human body, too, is a machine had a certain powerful attraction. This puzzle about anatomy was resolved by Harvey partly by appealing to analogies, to phenomena outside anatomy that were better understood. Nothing in the then-existing knowledge about these matters said or implied explicitly that the heart is a pump that circulates the blood; it was Harvey who said this, influenced by what was known at the time about the proper way of thinking about a variety of phenomena in anatomy and mechanics. That is, Harvey was guided in formulating his theory by the latent aspects of existing norms of thought in these areas. The microscope was soon invented, and in 1661 capillaries were found in the lungs of a frog. The materials were at hand to answer the question of how blood flowing away from the heart in the arterial system could get into the venous system to return to the heart. Anatomy could turn to the question of what was being carried by the blood in its circuit.[1]

II

A major theme in Will's work is the adverse consequences of the neglect of the importance of the latent aspect of norms of thought

❦

1. For a fascinating account of Harvey's discovery, see chapter 3 of Herbert Butterfield, *The Origins of Modern Science* (1965).

and action for our understanding of our intellectual practices. Philosophical accounts that countenance only the role of the manifest aspect of norms in our thinking fail notably to account for the growth of knowledge. The philosophical problems of skepticism about the knowledge of the external world and induction are insoluble, Will argues, without an explicit recognition of the role of the latent aspect of norms in their governance of our activity (1988, 47–63).

Similarly, norms pertaining to activities other than strictly theoretical ones, including moral norms, are not well understood when attention is focused entirely upon norms' manifest contents and their latent content is dismissed. Then, such norms tend to be thought of as simply explicit instructions that tell us what to do—hard-and-fast rules that provide explicit direction for every contingency. Of course, there are no such moral rules, but if the latent aspect of norms is neglected, then the only guidance that moral rules can provide is through what they explicitly direct. In fact, multiple moral considerations frequently indicate contrary courses of action in the same circumstances; moral norms conflict in particular situations. Sometimes it happens that the relevance of one or more norms is in doubt or is controversial. These and other problems are often unprecedented in some way. Moral norms, as a consequence, can offer no guidance where we are most in need of help, if we consider only their manifest content. A common response to this problem in moral philosophy is to seek very general and abstract principles that seem to be applicable in every situation—for example, the General Happiness Principle, the Golden Rule, or Kant's Formula of Humanity. A familiar difficulty with such abstract principles is that their application is problematic. Like the dicta of the Oracle at Delphi, what they have to say about a particular problem can be understood in more than one way. If we focus only on the manifest content of such abstract principles, their guidance is ambiguous.

Generally, Will maintains, norms of any kind cannot perform their guiding function when they are separated from their latent content—that is, when they are considered in abstraction from the actual contexts in which people attempt to live in accordance with them and the complex of other norms that pertain in the context. He cites Ludwig Wittgenstein's account in *Philosophical Investigations* (1953) of the necessity of a background of customary practice for a rule to have a clear meaning. Without such a background, Wittgenstein argues, any response can be made out to accord with a given rule, including continuing the series 2, 4, 6, 8, after reaching 1,000, by 1,004, 1,008, 1,012, and so on (1953, part I, sections 185–202).

> Similar glosses may be and have often been made upon other rules or norms that have been for certain philosophical purposes so abstracted from their latent content that they can no longer perform their expected guiding function. Strikingly similar in this aspect are many criticisms advanced against Kant's principle of universality in his Categorical Imperative, and, more recently, in Goodman's effective criticism of an abstract rule of inductive projection. In both these and many other cases a major point of the criticism is that embarrassingly many conflicting courses of action "can be made out to accord with the rule." (Will 1997, 165)

III

Will criticizes the attempts of philosophers to enunciate certain very general and abstract principles that are intended by means of their explicit content alone to indicate definitively the solution to complex intellectual and practical problems. For one thing, the procedures proposed do not indicate one particular solution; rather they point in several different directions at once. It appears, though, that a similar criticism can be made of Will's account of the way that the latent contents of norms guide us in the solution of difficult theoretical and practical problems. With respect to a given problem, the latent aspect of norms—that is, the larger social context of norm-rich accepted practice in which the problem arises—invariably indicates or suggests more than one solution. The vast body of norms here offers many different paradigms that might be brought to bear on the present problem. Norms in their latent aspect too often will not determine a single solution but rather offer suggestions for many incompatible solutions. This criticism is that the procedure is insufficiently determinate to offer the sort of guidance we seek with difficult problems that arise both in theory and practice.

If the aim in the end is conceived simply as making the entire collection of our many practices harmonious and mutually reinforcing as far as possible in the existing social context, there will seem to be more than one way to attain this result when two or more practical or theoretical considerations conflict in a particular problem. If in a particular circumstance, norm N_1 indicates that we do A, and norm N_2 indicates that we do B, where we can do either A or B but not both, then a proper solution to our problem would be to modify N_1 in such a way that it does not apply to this particular situation. Norms N_1 and N_2, then, would be more harmonious in that in circumstances like this, they will not conflict. The proper course of action here is B rather than A. We could just as well, however, modify norm N_2 instead of N_1, so that N_2 does not apply in the circumstance. This, too, would harmonize N_1 and N_2, but the result of this is that in the circumstance, we should do A rather than B. The latent content of norms apparently offers no way to choose between these alternatives. This is not the guidance we seek.

Consider, though, the problem of slavery as it confronted the people of the United States in the first half of the nineteenth century. Slavery existed as an institution in parts of the country; the fortunes of a substantial number of people were invested in slavery. At the same time, this institution existed in a political community that was deeply committed to liberal and egalitarian democratic social ideals. The conflict between the inequalities and cruelties of slavery and the political morality of this community in which slavery was practiced was acute. The conflict was eventually resolved, though at the cost of the appalling carnage of the Civil War, by abolishing slavery in all of the United States. Of course, the conflict could have been resolved the other way: the political and social morality could have been given up and the institution of slavery preserved. It is important to notice that in fact there were few (if any) proponents of the latter solution. What the pro-slavery faction wanted to do was, in effect, to preserve the situation of slavery in a democracy, with all its conflicts. There were attempts to establish that slaves were individuals who lacked certain features that entitled others to life, liberty, and the pursuit of happiness, but the differences these arguments alleged were doubtful. As the conflict continued and the political crisis drew near, pro-slavery people generally refused to permit discussion of the issue.

Giving up the norms of egalitarian political democracy was not seriously considered as an option in response to the slavery issue. The choice, as the participants saw it, was the continuation of a community (in some form) riven by the inconsistencies of slavery in a political democracy or a political democracy without slavery. In the circumstances, for these people, giving up the political democracy was unthinkable. No one was prepared to abandon the complex of norms that constitute life in a political democracy, and we do not need to postulate some mysterious intuition of the rightness of such a life to explain this. For one thing, political democracy is the best defense against tyranny, and these people knew it. The latent aspect of the social and political norms that defined political life in the United States in 1860 was not neutral on the issue of giving up slavery or giving up the political democracy.

If one reflects abstractly on the thesis that proper problem solving in theorizing and other activities is a matter of being guided by the latent aspect of norms, if one thinks about this proposal apart from concrete problems, it appears that the idea provides insufficient guidance. There will, it seems, be many more than one way of adjusting norms in conflict in a particular situation to the larger social and intellectual context in which the particular problem arises. The latent aspect of the pertinent norms will not seem to indicate a single solution to the problem. It seems here, too, that every course of action can be made to accord with the rule. When one considers particular concrete problems, however, the actual latent aspect of norms tends to be considerably more specific than this in its indication.

The mechanical model of the circulatory system, with the heart as a pump, is indicated in the seventeenth century by a number of considerations in anatomy and in the general culture. The Copernican heliocentric theory is indicated over the geocentric theory in the sixteenth century, not by any crucial experiment but because of the contemporary interest in astronomy as "a realistic representation of the structure of the solar system" rather than as a mere device for prediction and calculation (Will 1988, 243–45).

In fifteenth-century Europe, interest in trade and improvements in transportation created a demand for capital to finance commercial ventures. New nation-states fought wars, and rulers sought money to finance their wars. So eager were such individuals for capital that they were perfectly willing to pay others for the temporary use of their money. Lending at interest, however—usury—was viewed as a form of theft, a form of extorting from others property to which the lender has no just claim. By the end of the sixteenth century, casuists had reached a consensus that it was proper to lend money at interest, provided the interest was not excessive. The prohibition against lending at interest was modified to accommodate the insistent demand for capital, partly because the social and economic circumstances that originally gave moral meaning to the prohibition against lending at interest no longer obtained. In a subsistence economy, where wealth is not itself a commodity, idle goods are just that. When one's neighbor needs a loan, it is typically because the neighbor is in serious trouble. Charity indicates that one lend idle goods to a neighbor in difficulty, and one is entitled to ask for the eventual return of the principal. To make it a condition of the loan that the lender return more than the principal, however, is to extort additional property from the borrower—property to which the lender has no claim. Usury is theft.

When economic circumstances change so that idle capital can be invested to realize a profit, a lender can reasonably claim that the borrower owes compensation for lost profit in addition to the return of the principal. Potential borrowers, moreover, are eager for capital and perfectly willing to pay for its use. Lenders in such circumstances do not coerce the borrower to pay interest, and lenders have a claim to be entitled to more than the return of the principal. This was the situation in Europe in the sixteenth century. The latent aspect of the social and economic norms of the time indicated that the idea that lending money at interest is unjust be given up and replaced with the notion of reasonable interest (Jonsen and Toulmin 1988, chapter 9).

One may say that the casuists of the sixteenth century might just as well have held to the norm that lending at interest is unjust and demanded that princes and merchants restrain their lust for capital. The principle, however, had ceased to be morally cogent in the way it had once been. It is not reasonable to ask people to forgo exciting new ventures in the name of an ancient prohibition that has substantially lost its point.

In certain historical contexts, very general social and intellectual considerations indicate the proper solution to certain difficult unprecedented problems, even though no explicitly worked-out norms for dealing with such problems exist at the time. It is very particular features of the actual context, including the latent content of the existing norms, that rule out certain ways of harmonizing the norms directly involved in the problem and that indicate a preferable way of resolving the matter. To appreciate Will's point about the importance of the latent aspect of norms for providing guidance with unprecedented problems, one must attend to the particular social-historical situation. That is, one must think in terms of very concrete actual problems that have a context rich with particular circumstances that rule out some adjustments and indicate others. One must appreciate John Dewey's initially puzzling saying: "In quality, the good is never twice alike. It never copies itself. It is new every morning, fresh every evening. It is unique in its every presentation. For it marks the resolution of a distinctive complication of competing habits and impulses which can never repeat itself" (1922, 146).

IV

As long as one neglects the particular situation, it can seem that, inevitably, too many incompatible solutions to a problem will be consistent with the latent aspect of norms. Selected historical problems and their solutions help show that vexed problems can be uniquely and satisfactorily resolved with the help of their background complex of norms that constitute the social context in which the problem occurs.

It will seem to some, however, that in these historical examples, what is described as the proper resolution of problems with the guidance of the latent aspect of norms is simply the actual muddling-through that follows social and intellectual crises. Occasionally, more or less by chance, people hit on a good solution, a defensible one, in this way. This is not enough to show, the objection continues, that the people who "solved" the problem were guided by reliable problem-solving techniques. The concrete examples used above are nothing more than a selection of cases where things worked out well more or less by accident.

This objection is simply the claim that people are guided in their actions by intelligence or insight only when they follow norms whose manifest content indicates that they act as they do. One defense consists in arguing, as Will does, that the claim excludes too much that is paradigmatic of human intellectual excellence and success in both theoretical and practical domains.

The actual historical examples, however, are complex. Sometimes people are confronted by problems so unprecedented that there are no procedures that apply. The imagined case of the assembly-line worker who ran out of resistors of the proper value is an example of such a problem. It sometimes happens in the practical domain that social circumstances change so that a norm that was effective and important loses its point. There is sometimes an interval where the norm retains its adherents, even though it no longer serves its original function. Established norms can retain their hold over people even when the circumstances that gave those norms their point cease to obtain. When other concerns begin to clash with the outdated norm, it gradually yields, and people at the same time gradually become aware of the need for a modified norm. This process is often intermittent, confused, fumbling, halting, and only incompletely understood by the participants. Frequently, it is only when the process of change is in the later stages that anyone articulates at all clearly what is happening and why. The idea, clearly articulated, cannot be said to have guided the change. It does not seem implausible, however, to suppose that the idea, glimpsed unclearly and intermittently by the participants, played an important role in people's effecting the change.

European peoples in ancient times believed that the health, prosperity, and safety of their entire communities depended upon careful and faithful performance of specific religious observances. If the religious ceremonies were not properly observed, famine, plague, and other calamities were expected to result. It fell to the sovereign, whose function it was to serve and protect the general welfare of the community, to use all resources to ensure that the proper religious forms were observed. This was an important part of the job of protecting the public welfare. The notion that it was no part of the business of the state to concern itself with the most vigorous and strict maintenance of proper religious observances could find no acceptance in such circumstances. The details of proper observance of religious forms was a matter of the most urgent public interest.

Europeans gradually, over two or more millennia, ceased to accept the idea that impiety results in public calamity.

> Social changes, both intellectual and in the internal composition and external relations of peoples, took place so that men no longer connected attitudes of reverence or disrespect to the gods with the weal and woe of the community. Faith and unbelief still had serious consequences, but these were now thought to be confined to the temporal and eternal happiness of the persons directly concerned. Given the other belief, and persecution and intolerance are as justifiable as is organized hostility to any crime; impiety is the most dangerous of all threats to public peace and well-being. But social changes gradually effected as one of the new functions of the life of the community the rights of private conscience and creed. (Dewey 1927, 266–67)

It would be hard to exaggerate the historical importance in the history of the West of the development of the idea that religion is a private rather than a public matter. One of its consequences was the very gradual acceptance of a norm of civil toleration of religious diversity. Even after the Protestant Reformation, wars were fought and people cruelly persecuted in the name of religious orthodoxy. As the history of the Puritans in America shows, even those who had suffered from persecution were capable of practicing civil intolerance of religious diversity.

John Locke set out relatively clearly and concisely a case for civil toleration of religious diversity in his "A Letter Concerning Toleration." Written in Holland in 1685 and published in 1689, this letter argues that civil law, backed up with the sanction of coercive force, is an entirely inappropriate way to inculcate religious conviction. Civil power properly defends people's life, liberty, and property by impartial law and the threat of legal punishment; it is incompetent and inappropriate in religious matters.

> True and saving Religion consists in the inward perswasion of the Mind, without which nothing can be acceptable to God. And such is the nature of the Understanding, that it cannot be compell'd to the belief of any thing by outward force. Confiscation of Estate, Imprisonment, Torments, nothing of that nature can have any such Efficacy as to make Men change the inward Judgment that they have framed of things. (Locke 1689, 27)

Critics of Locke note that although there is an absurdity in the notion of attempting to coerce an individual into believing something, the idea of attempting to foster a certain belief in a community by suppressing public dissent and dissenters is not similarly absurd.[2] Locke's argument, though, is not best understood as an a priori argument against attempting to maintain religious orthodoxy by coercion. The force of his position emerges most clearly when he argues that religious officials should not attempt to extend their authority over civil matters. "The Church it self is a thing absolutely separate and distinct from the Commonwealth. The Boundaries on both sides are fixed and immovable. He jumbles Heaven and Earth together, the things most remote and opposite, who mixes these two Societies; which are in their Original, End, Business, and in every thing, perfectly distinct, and infinitely different from each other" (Locke 1689, 33).

The "End" of religion, as Locke conceives it, is the care of one's soul, a matter of "inward conviction." The function of the state, according to Locke, is to protect and foster the public good. These

---

2. See, for example, Jeremy Waldron, "Toleration and the Rationality of Persecution" (1991), 116–18. Contemporaries of Locke made this criticism, too. See also the account of Locke's controversy with Jonas Proast in Peter Nicholson, "John Locke's Later Letters on Toleration" (1991), 163–87.

things are "perfectly distinct." The subordination of one to the other is likely to be to the detriment of one or both. This line of argument makes very good sense against the background of the assumption that the public interest is not directly at stake in the matter of individuals' religious beliefs.

Long before the seventeenth century, most people had ceased to believe that departures from religious orthodoxy caused specific calamities such as war, famine, and pestilence. Yet the sense lingered that the public good was somehow at stake in religious matters. Norms that had lost their point through changes in people's beliefs and practices lingered beyond their term. Religious heterodoxy was a threat to the public order, people still felt. James I is reported to have said, "No Bishop, no King, no nobility" (Hill 1961, 1980, 65). Locke pointed out that as long as people in their religious practice do not violate civil laws designed to protect the public good, their acts and beliefs are not the business of the state. The matter is private rather than public.

In seventeenth-century England, church and state were complexly entangled, for historical reasons. It served the purposes of the ruling classes to appoint the clergy to their offices. For one thing, the pulpit was a crucially important means of communication in a country where many subjects were illiterate. It was advantageous in certain ways for the church that happened to be the state church to wield political power. Of course, the feeling lingered that somehow the public good depended crucially upon religious matters.

Increasingly, however, people who were serious about their religion conceived in the modern manner strove to practice and believe in ways that departed from the practice of the Church of England. In the dim past, it might have been possible to oppose such heterodoxy with the argument that specific calamities would befall the entire community if such practices were tolerated. Without this argument, however, the political-religious orthodoxy was unable to stem the fervor of dissenting Protestants and others. A social revolution was going on at the same time; an educated, energetic middle class strove with an entrenched aristocracy for political power. The religious and political revolutions were interconnected.

There were in Locke's time any number of reasons to support or oppose religious toleration and to except certain kinds of individuals from religious toleration: Charles II supported toleration because he desired to protect Catholics and seek alliance with France; certain contemporary Whigs favored toleration to protect dissident Protestants, and some merchants favored toleration because they perceived that their Dutch rivals' reputation for toleration gave the latter an advantage in trade (Cranston 1991, 79–80; Gough 1991, 58). Locke himself thought that the state should not tolerate atheists or Roman Catholics, because the former could not be trusted to keep oaths, while the latter owed allegiance to a foreign power (1689, 50–51).

The central point that Locke saw, however, is that religion and politics have very different purposes, and that the particular social practices for achieving those different purposes did not mesh well. The knowledge necessary for the effective pursuit of one of these ends did not qualify an individual for the effective pursuit of the other. The incursion of one practice into the domain of the other was apt to be at the expense of one or both. It may serve certain state ends to control appointments to religious offices so that political orthodoxy is preached from the pulpit, but religious officials appointed on such grounds are not necessarily qualified to serve their flock's religious needs.[3]

Priests who use political power to advance religious purposes, on one hand, are not primarily concerned with the public good. Rulers' worldly private interests are not the only things that might deflect them from the proper execution of their offices. The use of the coercive power of the state for determining matters of religious

---

3. See Michael Walzer's explanation of the wrongness of simony in *Spheres of Justice* (1983), 8–10. See, in addition, Walzer 1983, chapters 5 and 10.

doctrine, on the other hand, is no more appropriate than its use to determine matters of scientific theory, and for similar reasons. If one views the public good as consisting, at least in part, in the maintenance of circumstances in which important practices such as religion and science can flourish and participants can flourish in these practices, then it is so far not in the public interest for the state to attempt to influence by force the pursuit of these practices and the convictions of the practitioners. The exception is the circumstance where some aspect of such a practice presents a clear and present danger to the public.

A reader of Locke's *Second Treatise of Government* (1690) is struck by Locke's notion that much of the social activity that constitutes human life is governed by norms that are natural phenomena. So the family and the activities that take place in this domain are regarded as governed by natural law. Work, commerce, and property are likewise natural phenomena, social features of the "state of nature." Religion, too, appears to be possible in the state of nature. Civil government, unlike most of the other important social institutions and practices he discusses, he held to be artificial—a human creation for human purposes. The notion that certain social practices are natural rather than artificial is untenable, for reasons that Hume tried to articulate, but this does not invalidate Locke's account of the functions and interrelationships of these various institutions.[4]

Locke had a very strong sense of the diverse functions of certain social practices and institutions, and he saw clearly that the coercive powers of the state, however important for certain purposes, were ill-suited for regulating the internal functioning of certain other

---

4. Some modern critics deny that we can ascertain the function of social practices and institutions, but little in the way of argument is offered for the denial. See Waldron 1991, 100–101. If we can ascertain the function of such artifacts as carpenters' tools, there is nothing in principle to prevent us from ascertaining the functions of our social artifacts.

important practices, particularly religion. He articulated this insight more or less clearly in 1685, after a substantial degree of religious liberty had been realized in England. He saw that religion had become a matter of individuals' spiritual welfare and salvation in accordance with their convictions concerning what God required. This, and not the preservation of the community from calamity, was religion's "End." What Locke articulated, however, was something of which others had been more or less aware for some time. Those who have a sense of what religion conceived in the modern way is about and who care about this are apt to resist the incursion of politics into religion. Those who at the same time keep before themselves a lively sense of the purpose of the exercise of political power in the public interest and who properly appreciate how easily rulers are distracted from their proper concern will resist the use of such power for religious ends. They may describe their reasons for such resistance in various ways, or they may be unable to articulate them at all. They see in their existing activities a compelling need for a norm of religious tolerance, and gradually they adopt it and refine it.

A norm of civil toleration of religious diversity developed as religion and politics developed. Such historical developments are rarely clearly seen and understood by those involved in them. They catch glimpses of the developing norm only fleetingly and they struggle to articulate it. It may seem to them that they are only discovering something that was there all along, when in fact they are participating in the norm's creation, if only in a confused and subconscious way.

V

We are familiar with the distinction between the letter and the spirit of the law. Frederick Will explicitly identifies the latent aspect of norms with what he calls the "spirit" or the "will" of the body of norms that pertain to some important activity, institution, or enterprise (1997, 183, 187). When the explicit, manifest content of the rules, principles, instructions, or lore that people have articulated in developing and teaching a certain practice do not provide direction for coping with a certain problem, they can still look to the norms of the practice and its social context for direction. They can look to the "spirit" of the undertaking.

This is apt to strike us as mysterious. The idea of appeal to the spirit or will of a collection of principles seems to invite idiosyncratic responses, caprice, and chaos—the very opposite of objective rational determination. We are familiar, however, with the contrast between what we want in a certain situation, on one hand, and what the situation calls for or demands, on the other. It is the latter that is the objective determination to which our desires must yield if they conflict with it, if we are to respond reasonably and properly. Perhaps situations demand only metaphorically (though the metaphor is more dead than alive); it is no more than a natural extension of this familiar way of talking and thinking, however, to attribute spirits and wills to situations. It follows, then, that the will or spirit of a situation that confronts us with a problem has a certain objective force that endows its demands with authority. One may not want to talk about the will or spirit of a certain collection of norms, but there can be no doubt that there is such a thing. In complex matters, what the spirit or will of the enterprise indicates may be difficult to discern, especially for those implicated in the problem, but this is to be attributed to complexity, the limited capacities of human beings, and the difficulty of understanding matters as one participates in them. In such circumstances, Will says, "the superiority of any reading of the spirit...is something that often can only be guessed at and can be determined with assurance only by the way in which one or other competitor succeeds in effecting a resolution of the conflict that originally gave rise to the governing activity" (1997, 189–90).

John Locke understood that government and religion, as he knew these complex phenomena, had diverse purposes that properly were pursued and fostered by very different means requiring different abilities and competences. Assuming that the flourishing of religious activity contributes to the good of the community, Locke argued, in effect, that in order for government to fulfill its purpose of regulating individuals for the common good, government should not intrude into purely religious matters. The state should protect the autonomy of the religious sphere. The force of the position comes from the historical circumstances. Religion, once conceived of as a community's ritual techniques for appeasing the gods and warding off calamities, had increasingly become a matter of individuals' ways of tending their own individual spiritual needs. It was no longer possible to justify the hardships and cruelty resulting from civil coercion to maintain religious orthodoxy by the argument that only by such means can community disaster be averted. Once religion becomes primarily a matter of individual salvation, such desperate measures are without justification. Coercion in religion seems unnecessary and, given the kind of enterprise religion had become, counterproductive. This change in the understanding of the point and focus of religion, this metamorphosis in the spirit of the religious enterprise, was more the cause than the effect of Protestantism (Dewey 1927, 266–67). Locke often wrote about such matters as though he were discovering natural rights that had existed all along. The right of privacy in religious matters was a right that could be discovered, however, only when religion had become a private rather than a public matter.

Despite what he may have thought, Locke was not announcing in his letter the discovery of an eternal, unchanging natural right. Neither, however, was he simply proclaiming his own or his class's preferences about the relationship of church and state. Locke was articulating what the social situation indicated with respect to this vexed matter, given that the practice and understanding of religion and of government had changed in a fundamental way. The spirit or will of the enterprise of religion in its altered form indicated that religion be understood as distinct and very different from government. Nothing explicitly said that. Certain existing practices, moreover, together with the persistence of cultural commitment to the idea that religious diversity was tantamount to anarchy, resisted such a new norm. Those individuals who cared about religion as a matter of personal salvation and those who took seriously the notion that government's function is to foster, not to impede, the pursuit of important practices that constitute the life of the community, supported the civil toleration of religious diversity. They spoke and acted objectively as the spirit of the enterprise indicated, as the situation demanded.

VI

The assumption in much philosophical thinking in all areas of philosophy that norms of thought and action guide us only by means of the specific direction provided by their manifest contents has the result that they offer no help in sufficiently novel situations. Efforts to discover or construct norms that explicitly indicate the proper course in every circumstance prove futile. Indeed, how could they succeed? We have no way of knowing of any particular norm that it will explicitly indicate the right response in circumstances we cannot now anticipate. The recognition of the importance of the latent aspect of norms for constructive thinking about vexed intellectual and practical problems provides a way out of this impasse. The value of Will's account lies not only in the very considerable intellectual satisfaction of this insight. The way is cleared and the direction is indicated for philosophical work that promises constructive contributions to the discussion of the most important problems we face.

THREE *Social Artifacts and Ethical Criticism*

It is difficult for many philosophers to accept the idea that norms, including ethical norms, are fundamentally constituents of actual practices. The view seems to them to conceive norms in such a way that the norms cannot perform effectively their most important function—providing standards for the rigorous criticism of actual practice. The view is thought, at best, to engender an unacceptably conservative posture toward existing social and political arrangements, a bias toward the status quo. At the very worst, the view will seem to provide a superabundance of conflicting norms with no way to adjudicate among them.

In fact, the view that norms are constituents of practices is not inherently socially conservative, nor, for that matter, is it necessarily radically critical. It is compatible with the deep reverence toward tradition of an Edmund Burke and with the arguments for extensive social change of a John Dewey or a Michael Walzer. The complex structures of norms that constitute practices provide ample critical resources for the examination and appreciation of existing practices and for their reform where indicated. The plurality of norms guarantees that they will conflict with one another. In the abstract, the appeal to the norms themselves to resolve such conflicts appears unpromising, but attention to the social-historical contexts in which the conflicts arise brings the latent aspects of the norms into view.

Here is the ground on which to stand to defend proposals for the alteration and adaptation of norms.

The assumption that sufficiently searching and stringent criticism of intellectual and other practices requires that we employ norms of criticism that are independent of actual practices has a long history in philosophy. Plato's theory of forms is an early example of a philosophical attempt to conceive norms as independent in this way. So, too, are the natural law of the Stoics and of later philosophers and various Enlightenment conceptions of moral standards as eternal truths that reveal themselves to the natural light of reason or intuition. This search for practice-independent norms that will end disagreement has led in fact to much philosophical disagreement. The philosophical difficulties surrounding these and other attempts to formulate such norms and account for their origin and authority are well known. Upon surveying the long series of unsuccessful attempts, it would be reasonable to conclude that the program of understanding norms as independent of practices is infeasible. It is only the assumption that there *must* be such practice-independent norms if searching criticism is to be possible, I suspect, that sustains philosophers in their unrewarded search for such things. Philosophers committed to the position that there must be such independent norms if searching criticism of practices is to be possible are thus sustained in their labors.

My aim is to make plausible the idea that developed human practices can be effectively criticized by norms that are constituents of them—that practices are in that sense self-criticizing—in order to circumvent a large area of vexed philosophical struggle and controversy. The idea of self-criticizing practices exists in the work of Peirce and Dewey; a more recent development of the view is by Frederick L. Will (1988 and 1997, 159–92). One sees hints of such a view elsewhere. If such criticism is possible, we should be able to exhibit clear examples of actual criticism of social practice in terms of norms internal to practices, criticism that is cogent and constructive. In fact, this type of criticism turns out to be complicated. Instances of contemporary criticism invite disagreement, because we are considering matters that for us lie within an area of uncertainty and controversy. We must exhibit social criticism that we can agree (1) appeals to norms that are internal to our practices, and (2) is clearly effective social criticism. The best argument against the claim that such criticism is impossible is to produce clear examples of just that thing.

The writings of the historian and political philosopher Michael Walzer are a good place to look for this sort of criticism. Not only is Walzer a vigorous social critic, he has written extensively about social criticism. In *Interpretation and Social Criticism* he is explicit about how he conceives the social character of the norms to which he appeals.

> Every human society provides for its members—they provide for themselves through the medium of justification—standards of virtuous character, worthy performance, just social arrangements. The standards are social artifacts; they are embodied in many different forms: legal and religious texts, moral tales, epic poems, codes of behavior, ritual practices.... [The social critic's principles] are only apparently external; they are really aspects of the same collective life that is perceived to require criticism. (Walzer 1987, 47–48)

I

For example, in *Spheres of Justice* (1983), Walzer argues that distributive justice is not determined by one or even a few abstract general principles. People distribute a great many different sorts of things: "membership, power, honor, ritual eminence, divine grace, kinship and love, knowledge, wealth, physical security, work and leisure, rewards and punishments, and a host of goods more narrowly and materially conceived—food, shelter, clothing, transportation, medical care, commodities of every sort, and all the odd things...that human beings collect" (Walzer 1983, 3). How they properly distribute such things, Walzer maintains, is determined in each case by how they collectively think about that particular kind of thing. The goods that are distributed by a group of people have "social meanings" that are given to them by those people. We make the goods, Walzer says, we give them their meanings. The social meaning of a good is an important determinant of how the good is properly distributed. "Distributions are patterned in accordance with shared conceptions of what the goods are and what they are for." "If we understand what it is, what it means to those for whom it is a good, we understand how, by whom, and for what reasons it ought to be distributed" (Walzer 1983, 7, 9).

Walzer illustrates these points by many historical examples. For instance, there was for a time a practice of selling offices in the medieval Christian church. One could become rector of a religious house or congregation, a bishop, or a cardinal by paying a sum of money. This practice came to be called "simony" and was found to be improper, sinful. Walzer says, "Given the Christian understanding of office, it followed—I am inclined to say it necessarily followed—that office holders should be chosen for their knowledge and piety and not for their wealth" (1983, 9). Medieval Christians found that their shared conception of what church office is and what it is for—tending the spiritual needs of a certain community of people—indicates that qualifications such as knowledge and piety and not wealth and a willingness to pay are the proper basis for distributing office. Church offices are not properly commodities to be bought and sold in the marketplace. Distributing church offices as commodities violates the meaning of such offices.

The meaning that church office had for Christians was implicated in the Christian church and the role that this institution played in their lives. Walzer talks of the "logic" of institutions. Given what the Christian church was—a complex social practice with an understood spiritual function and purpose—such qualifications as knowledge and piety were strongly indicated as the basis for allocating church offices. The meaning that church office had for these people was a shared social meaning, but their agreement was conditioned by the religious practice they shared. The norm of distribution indicated by their shared understanding of the meaning of office was in this way an integral part of their religious practice; it was an aspect of a social artifact. Of course, some Christians at that time in fact treated offices as commodities to be exchanged for money, and so this was their practice, too. It may well have been that at least some of those who bought and sold offices saw nothing wrong in this. Whether these people knew it or not, however, what they were doing in practicing simony was deeply subversive of the purpose of the church as they all understood it. "The same men and women who act badly," Walzer says, "create and sustain the standards by which (at least sometimes) they know themselves to act badly" (1987, 48). We can imagine changes in the medieval church that would have removed the elements of religious practice that were discordant with the sale of church offices. Such changes, however, would alter the institution in ways that would have been completely unacceptable to Christians. Its character as the sort of spiritual community it aspired to be (and to a degree was) would not survive such a change. The norm that indicated that offices should be allotted on the basis of spiritual qualifications was indeed required by the logic of the institution, by the latent content of its constituent norms.

Similarly, Walzer says, markets are arenas where people come together to exchange commodities freely to satisfy their many diverse desires. Our understanding of this practice conditions our understanding of wealth—what wealth is for and why it matters. The proposal that wealth be continually and forcibly redistributed to realize and sustain a simple equality of possessions among members of society would subvert the point of wealth and markets. In this sense, the shared social meaning of commodities and markets rules out the propriety of such systems for equal distributions (Walzer 1983,

107–8). For similar reasons, the character of practices and the shared social meanings of related goods indicate that prestige cannot properly be distributed equally to everyone, and that honors and prizes cannot be distributed on the basis of recipients' need.

It is not just the isolated fact that people in a certain community happen to share certain beliefs about church office and wealth that accounts for the norms about how these are properly distributed. It is their shared beliefs about what role office or wealth plays in an important area of their life. They agree not only in what they think but also in what they do and how they live. Of course, they disagree, too. Their shared beliefs about the meaning of a good are thoroughly and complexly related to their shared practice with respect to that good. It is their practice with respect to the good that gives the good its meaning. Walzer's account of justice depends upon the idea that the norms that govern distributions are integral components of practices.

On the basis of such a view, Walzer criticizes current practice in the United States with respect to medical care. Our current distribution of medical care, he argues, falls short of what is required by our shared understanding of the meaning of such provision. The argument in outline is this. A central purpose of a political community is to provide for the security and welfare of its members. What sort of provision is needed and how much is a matter for political decision, but the members of a democratic political community will have an obligation to provide equally for citizens in proportion to their needs (Walzer 1983, 84). For good historical reasons, medical care has come to be regarded as an extremely important need of every person. It has attained a level of importance as an individual need comparable to the need for security from attack from within and without, old-age pensions, and education. The importance our community assigns to health as a need is reflected in the very extensive community provisions for public health, hospitals, medical research, medical education, and care for the aged and indigent. Our commitment to provide "minimally decent health care for all who need it" is further evidenced by the fact that the very sick and the very old often receive medical treatment at public expense. We fail, though, to provide equally adequate medical care for all our fellow citizens who need it. The system of free enterprise in medical care that exists in the United States tends to provide care on the basis of ability to pay rather than need for care. Because of the high cost of medical care, the result is very unequal provision of medical care for the members of our community, and this is a failure to fulfill our commitment to provide medical care to all equally on the basis of need. The remedy, Walzer says, is to turn a substantial number of physicians into public employees and to constrain the market in medical care (1983, 86–90).

This is another example of social criticism that appeals to norms that are components of existing practice. To the extent that the criticism is cogent, it serves as a counterexample to the claim that if moral and other norms are conceived as components of actual practices, searching social criticism is impossible. It challenges the prejudice that such a view of norms is objectionably biased toward the status quo or that it renders the norms ineffective for criticism.

Walzer's argument for our commitment to the public provision of medical care has in fact been severely criticized. The criticism poses the issues sharply. Walzer, according to Joshua Cohen, is faced with what Cohen calls "the simple communitarian dilemma": "If the values of a community are identified through its current distributive practices, then the distributive norms subsequently 'derived' from those values will not serve as criticisms of existing practices.... [I]f we identify values apart from practices, with a view to assessing the conformity of practices to those values, what evidence will there be that we have the values right?" (1986, 463–64)

Current arrangements in the United States for the distribution of medical care do reflect conflicting ideas about what is proper in this area. Walzer manages to criticize aspects of our current arrangements for the distribution of medical care, Cohen charges, by selecting certain aspects of current practice and values and ignoring others. Walzer's criticisms of current practices, Cohen claims, rest on "arbitrary and tendentious descriptions of 'our' values." For example, Walzer claims that our commitment of public funds to medical care shows our recognition that health care is a need, that we intend to provide minimally decent care to all who need it. In fact, though, Cohen argues, health care in the United States is largely private and unequally provided. Why, Cohen asks, is this not also data about our conception of health care? "It is not at all clear," he says, "how Walzer's interpretation fits these data, and, if it does not, why it is legitimate to disregard them" (1986, 464).

Cohen and Walzer agree on the salient facts about actual practice: we sometimes treat health care as a matter of publicly supported welfare provision properly distributed on the basis of need and sometimes as a commodity distributed on the basis of the ability to pay for it. Our actual practice exemplifies two different principles of distribution of health care and two different conceptions of the nature of medical care—welfare need and commodity. Nothing in these social circumstances, according to Cohen, indicates any reason to regard one kind of distribution of health care as proper and the other as improper. The general point that Cohen is making in his criticism is that if we regard actual practice as itself normative, we must either accept *all* practice as proper, or we must appeal to norms that have a basis outside of practice. Since Walzer rejects the notion of norms external to practice, he has no basis for accepting some aspects of actual practice as exemplifying the proper way of distributing health care and rejecting other aspects of practice as improper, unjust.

Walzer's interpretation of our current practices with respect to health care and their related norms and values, however, is stoutly defended by a historical argument that does, in fact, countenance the current widespread understanding of medicine as free enterprise and reject that aspect of our practice as wrong. He argues that the conception of health care as a commodity now persists even though the social-historical circumstances that once provided its basis no longer obtain. Crucial to Walzer's argument is an account of how changes in certain practices alter for us the character and importance of the goods that the practices serve. The view that physicians are entrepreneurs who properly provide a marketable commodity does indeed have currency in the United States. The view of medical practice as free enterprise grew up in earlier times when physicians could do relatively little to ease the suffering and prevent the deaths of most seriously ill or injured people. Too often, the only attitude that people could take then toward their serious health problems was stoical acceptance. The attendance of a physician, at best, might offer some comfort to those willing and able to pay for it. This was hard, but it was the human condition. Over the last century, effective medical means have increasingly become widely available to ease suffering and prolong lives in a great many cases. It is now often the case that a person with a painful and/or life-threatening medical condition can be successfully treated. With such help widely available, people cannot be expected simply to accept suffering and death because they lack the money to buy medical care. For us to stand by and watch our fellow citizens suffer and die for lack of health care in the present state of medical technology has become like standing by and watching a neighbor die for lack of shelter or police protection. The claim that medical care *has become* in the last few decades, because of its increased effectiveness, a need as important, urgent, and morally compelling as police protection and education is not arbitrary or tendentious. That medical care is now a need of such consummate importance to everyone that it calls for community provision can be argued by calling attention, as Walzer does, to its present similarity in urgency to other needs for which we already think public provision is necessary.

Walzer does not ignore the fact that many Americans do view medical care simply as a commodity. In fact, he explicitly argues that this view, once more or less appropriate, is now outmoded. The arguments of the guild of physicians for their entrepreneurial prerogatives (or today the claims of the private health insurance industry and pharmaceutical companies for profits for their investors) are now far outweighed by the manifest urgency of reliable equal provision of an adequate level of modern medical care to all members of the community who need it. The existing extensive support from public resources of health care evidences our recognition of its importance as a need. It is no longer appropriate to think of health care simply as a commodity to be exchanged in the marketplace. Social-historical conditions that once made such a practice acceptable have changed, so that the practice is no longer appropriate (Walzer 1983, 86–91).

Walzer's argument that health care should be distributed equally on the basis of need is like his argument that church offices should be distributed on the basis of knowledge and piety, in that he explicitly considers in each case actual practices in their social-historical context. He thus appeals to what Frederick Will called the latent aspects of norms conceived as components of actual practices. So, in medieval times simony was a practice, but it was a practice in conflict with an already existing complex practice that constituted the Christian church. Taking account of the social-historical circumstances, it was clear that it was the practice of simony that was improper—it violated the meaning of the very offices that it distributed. Walzer likewise argues that the practice of treating needed medical care as a commodity conflicts with our best understanding in the present circumstances of the kind of thing health care is. A difference between the cases is that whereas treating church offices as commodities was always improper, treating medical care as a commodity was once proper and became improper only when medicine developed to the point where it could reliably and effectively serve extremely important human needs. Because of the high cost of modern medical care, distributing it on the basis of the ability to pay will not distribute it to many who urgently need it. In a community that tries to make public provision for needs of comparable urgency, treating health care as a commodity to the extent we do is bad practice.

Walzer's claims about our practices and values with respect to health care are defended by arguments based upon a plausible historical understanding of those practices. Those claims are not, as Cohen claims, "arbitrary and tendentious." The actual practices of a community are properly viewed in relation to one another and in their relationship to historical circumstances that are continually changing. Practices and their constituent norms sometimes persist even when circumstances that called for them have ceased to obtain. The persistence in the United States of the idea that medical care is simply a commodity that is properly distributed on the basis of people's ability to pay is the persistence of a practice that has lost its rationale. Too many people continue to hold to the idea, more or less oblivious or indifferent to its increasing obsolescence and the moral and social cost of its maintenance.

The sort of argument that Walzer offers rejects not only the premise that in searching social criticism, we must appeal to norms that are independent of actual practices, but it also rejects the assumption that the meaning of our practices and values is always transparent to us. In other words, Walzer supposes that it is possible for us to be mistaken about the norms and values that are actually indicated by our practices, and, he assumes, the way we act may be premised upon such misunderstanding. Walzer is not talking only about imposed misunderstandings, "false consciousness" due to the "lies, humbug, and polluted speech" of clever and powerful manipulators (Williams 1985, 101–2). Our practices are enormously complex. We do not always see clearly their character and their relationships to one another and to historical change and development. When we consider such actual practices as our provision for security and welfare in the United States—the "sphere" of security and welfare, Walzer calls it—or the practice of medicine in our country at present, it is not implausible to claim that even intelligent participants might misunderstand such social artifacts.

Ethical debate in a community over a period of time has sometimes taken the form of a gradual, painful realization that formerly important norms that significantly structured people's lives have lost their rationale and point. In such circumstances, some people continue to cling passionately for a time to the obsolete norms. So, in the sixteenth century, some Europeans continued to hold to the idea that lending money at interest—"usury"—was always a form of extortionate theft, despite the development of economic conditions that rendered money itself a commodity that many people were eager to buy (Jonsen and Toulmin 1988, chapter 9). The idea that the state has a compelling reason to enforce a strict religious orthodoxy persisted in England and elsewhere in the seventeenth century, even though the original rationale—the idea that strict observance of religious forms is necessary to prevent such public calamities as drought, famine, and plague—had been abandoned many centuries before (Dewey 1927, 266–67). Thus, John Locke could argue in 1689 that religion is largely a private matter in which the guardian of the public interest, the state, usually has no compelling interest (1689). Still, many of Locke's contemporaries continued to think that the state, in some way that they could not clearly articulate, has an important stake in enforcing religious orthodoxy.

Joshua Cohen, from the perspective of the long practice of philosophers, takes the existence of conflicting practices, norms, and values in a community as posing an insoluble difficulty for the view that moral norms are constituents of practices. Where there are conflicting practices or norms, he argues, the proponents of the practices in conflict give different interpretations of what the prevailing social situation indicates about what our practices, norms, and values mean. Walzer has to maintain that only one of these interpretations is correct. "That is, [Walzer has to maintain that] only one [interpretation] captures the values that we *really* share. But Walzer gives no *content* to the claim that one member of a set of competing interpretations, each of which fits our institutions and practices, might still be the right one. Beyond fitting the way of life in our community, there are no further constraints to be satisfied" (Cohen 1986, 466).

Consider the possibility, though, that Cohen is looking in the wrong place for the relevant "constraints." He asks, in effect: when people in a community understand their practices and values differently and disagree about them, and when these various understandings are reflected in what people actually do, how can we characterize one of these different understandings as *their shared* understanding, as *the correct* understanding of what they do? Posed abstractly in this way, the question invites the answer that there apparently is no single shared understanding; we cannot decide which understanding is correct as long as we regard the actual practices themselves as the only standards of correctness.

To support his claim about what our values are and what they indicate about how medical care should be distributed, however, Walzer points to features of a particular social-historical situation: the politics of security and welfare and the provision of health care in the United States in the late twentieth century. He appeals, in effect, to the latent content of these norms and practices. It is a complex situation: at the same time that people are participating in politics and medicine, they are participating in and pursuing a plurality of goods. In their practice, they are guided by norms that are shaped by their understanding of how they can deal effectively with their world. They must fulfill their many needs and pursue their various different purposes by practicing effectively and by practicing harmoniously with one another. Their understanding of how best to do all these things is itself a result of their collective experience, their history of encounters with their world. They are living in and through social artifacts that they, as individuals, found when they came upon the scene. Their understanding of these practices and how the practices interrelate is more or less inadequate. These artifacts, moreover, were and are more or less imperfect, more or less ineffective in realizing their purposes, and more or less discordant with other indispensable practices. When participants in such a life encounter a challenging practical problem, the case for solving their problem by careful attention to the concrete social-historical situation in which it occurs is compelling. It is quixotic to attempt to resolve the problem by manipulating concepts in the abstract, by attending only to the manifest content of the pertinent norms and overlooking their latent content due to the actual social context.

The preceding sketch of our existing social world and how practical problems should be resolved by attending to the particular context in which the problems arise is itself very general and, in its way, abstract. The sketch does not by itself imply that we owe to one another an equal provision for needed medical care. It does imply, though, that our practices need continual scrutiny and criticism, and that the practices themselves and their particular social-historical situation offer rich resources for interpretation and criticism. It is the complex structure of the actual social-historical situation, including our commitments and practices, our continual disagreements, and the actual possibilities that the particular situation allows that provides the substance and the constraints for the argument. Walzer supports his criticisms of our provision of medical care by reference to our particular history and circumstances. He argues about these matters as a historically oriented philosopher should.

Conflict and change characterize any actual social situation. The pursuit of one good tends to conflict with the pursuit of another, and people in a community pursue a great many different goods. Where people are able to resolve such conflicts successfully, thereby changing and harmonizing their practices, their success is apt to be temporary. Changing circumstances will disrupt the harmony, or new conflicts will emerge. Controversy and disagreement accompany such developments. There is an understandable philosophical urge to stand aside from the apparent chaos, to try to resolve the conflicts and controversies by appeal to abstract considerations that do not depend upon particular social-historical "contingencies." It is assumed that this is the only recourse in response to actual deep disagreements about moral and political matters (Rawls 1993, 1996, 43–46). In the abstract, though, it seems obvious that we cannot take a sufficiently critical attitude toward our practices as long as our critical resources are implicated in those practices themselves. It is only when we consider concrete issues in the context of thick particular social artifacts that we see the sufficiency of effective critical resources those practices offer us. By turning away from actual practices in their historical contexts in a search for external norms, philosophers lose sight of the very thing that makes criticism possible, the latent content of actual norms and practices.

The idea of a "reflective equilibrium" between a theory and the beliefs it is designed to explain has been current in the philosophy of science for some time. According to this idea, a harmonious adjustment between theory and beliefs is properly attained by modifying both theory and beliefs in a sort of back-and-forth dialectic to attain harmonious equilibrium. In principle, on this conception, nothing is immune from alteration if necessary to attain the desired harmonious consistency. John Rawls introduced the idea of reflective equilibrium into ethical theorizing (1971, 1999, 18–19). It has also been noticed that proper critical adjustment of theories and particular beliefs must take account of and accommodate the larger social-intellectual context in which the critical enterprise is situated. This enlarged conception of critical adjustment that takes into account "background beliefs and theories" as well as theory and its subject matter has been given the name "wide reflective equilibrium" (Daniels 1996; Benjamin 2003, 112–22). In arguing about health care, Walzer seeks something akin to wide reflective equilibrium among judgments about what justice requires in the distribution of medical care, practices with respect to medical care, and the social-historical context in which these issues arise.

Controversy and disagreement recur at the abstract level in the arguments of philosophers, too often in ways that seem irrelevant to people who grapple with hard practical problems. The judgment of Isaiah Berlin is relevant.

> One cannot have everything, in principle as well as in practice—and if human creativity may depend upon a variety of mutually exclusive choices: then, as Chernyshevsky and Lenin once asked, "What is to be done?" How do we choose between possibilities? What and how much must we sacrifice to what? There is, it seems to me, no clear reply. But the collisions, even if they cannot be avoided, can be softened. Claims can be balanced, compromises can be reached: in concrete situations not every claim is of equal force....The concrete situation is almost everything. (Berlin 1988, 17, 18)

The character of norms as components of actual practices is not widely recognized and understood. Critical ethical debate has gone on and does go on despite this failure to understand. My claim is that a better philosophical understanding of what we are doing in ethical and social criticism and of the nature of the norms to which we appeal would help us conduct our critical discussions more constructively and effectively. I am not claiming that those who conceive of norms as independent of actual practice have nothing useful to say about ethical problems. After all, we do not need to share the utilitarian view of Peter Singer, the natural law perspective of John Finnis, or the Rawlsian conception of Norman Daniels to benefit from their critical discussions of ethical problems. To the extent that one disagrees with their basic philosophical perspectives, one will approach their discussions with caution. One may expect that their arguments would be better if they had a different philosophical perspective. One nevertheless reasonably hopes and expects to benefit from their writings. I approach the discussions of those who suppose they are appealing to practice-independent norms in a similar spirit. I would not recommend readers' canceling their subscriptions to *Philosophy and Public Affairs.*

In this chapter, I have argued, in opposition to the claim that effective social and ethical criticism requires appeal to practice-independent norms, that social criticism is carried on effectively by appeal to norms that are internal to practices. I have exhibited and discussed specimens of such criticism. There are many other such specimens throughout this book. I have shown that the objection that actual practice is too variable and conflicting to enable such criticism fails. Furthermore, conceiving of norms as practice-independent directs our attention away from the latent aspect of norms that is so crucial to understanding and criticism. Viewing norms as components of actual practices that have a history, by contrast, brings this crucial aspect of norms clearly to the fore.

The view that practices and the norms they comprise are the result of the historical experience of people living together in particular circumstances reveals the empirical character of the knowledge ethics studies. We all to a greater or lesser degree have this practical knowledge. We, therefore, have access to this know-how as participants in the practices, and what we have access to is normative. We are not limited in our investigations of the practices to observing these practices as outsider-anthropologists (Ebbs 1997, 247–52). At the same time, this practical knowledge is so close to us that it is often difficult to see it clearly. The complexity and interconnectedness of the practices that make up our lives further add to the difficulty, so that strenuous effort may be required in order to articulate clearly what we know and to describe accurately the uses of such knowledge.

The phenomenon of the participant perspective is found in all areas of practical knowledge. So, if I wonder how a certain operation with a tool is properly done, if I know how to work with the tool, then I may well be able to find out successfully how this particular operation is properly done simply by reflecting on how I would do the operation. So cooks generally know when risen dough is ready for baking, English speakers know proper word order in sentences, and physicians know to wash their hands after seeing a patient. It is not always necessary for people who have the perspective of a participant to observe other practitioners to satisfy themselves about how things are properly done, though they may be prudent to consult other practitioners for confirmation. Further, having mastered a practice and thus being in possession of a complex body of practical knowledge is not the same as being able to articulate what one knows. Individuals competent in the same practice sometimes disagree in their characterizations of the nature and uses of the practice. It is only necessary to consider what (to mention only a few of many examples) artists, Supreme Court justices, and philosophers sometimes say about what they are doing to appreciate this point. The misconceptions that lie behind some of these pronouncements can have a deleterious effect upon how people actually practice.

The perspective of the participant seems to provide a special sort of access to normative practical knowledge. This is consistent, however, with the practical knowledge itself being empirical knowledge. The knowledge of how to work with the tool is based upon the actual practical experience of one or more people who have used it and discovered thereby how it is best used. Philosophers today sometimes appeal to the perspective of the participant in ethics when they consult what they call their "intuitions" about particular ethical questions. What they are accessing from this perspective, however, is actually the knowledge they have as participants in a life structured by ethical norms. The knowledge they have as participants is knowledge based on the experience of many people. This normative practical knowledge is thus fundamentally a posteriori, based on experience. If a priori means independent of experience, then it is a mistake to treat moral knowledge as a priori. We should turn away from certain abstract theories of ethics and look instead at the practical knowledge that is the precipitate of the experience of those who came before us and is our resource for living together intelligently and well.

It is important in understanding the practical knowledge we have now to consider its place and function in the present social-historical context and, where we can, its historical antecedents. An appropriate part of the philosophical investigation of ethics, then, is the study of particular historical examples that show the actual development of social artifacts and exhibit people's use of practices' constituent norms in solving problems. Health care in the United States is a case in point. Fictional examples developed in detail by novelists can also provide philosophically illuminating examples of the use of ethical norms in complex, richly described contexts, as in Martha Nussbaum's discussions in *Love's Knowledge* of works by Henry James, Charles Dickens, and others (1990). Throughout this book, I consider many such examples, both historical and fictional. These examples are offered as evidence for the claims I make about ethical norms and how they are best studied.

II

Norms that are components of actual practices can and do provide for searching, effective social criticism. The proponent of practice-independent ethical norms may acknowledge this point and still consistently maintain that there are practice-independent norms, but the argument that there *must* be such norms for effective criticism is undercut. When important norms are conceived as practice-independent, moreover, they are abstracted from their social-historical contexts, the actual complex of practices that provides their latent meanings. In view of the long history of endless disagreement about the nature, source, and authority of practice-independent norms, the idea of such norms should be abandoned in philosophy.

It is sometimes important for us to be able to criticize the practices and institutions of communities other than our own, to advocate reforms in other lands. If the only critical standards available to us were the norms implicit in the practices in the community being criticized, it would still be possible to argue that the community was not living up to its own standards when in fact it was not doing so. So, we can argue that the practice of simony in medieval times was wrong by their values, or someone from another community can argue that our tendency to treat medical care as a commodity is wrong by our own standards. We could also argue that the practices of another community fail by *our* standards, but why should we expect that this will matter to those who do not share our practices and norms? We are moved to advocate reform in other communities when we find their practices unsatisfactory in certain ways, but for our advocacy of reform in other communities to make a difference to them, we must appeal to norms that have currency with the members of the other community. Universal ethical norms that hold everywhere independent of the existing practices of any community could provide the standards for cross-cultural social criticism, so it appears that we still have reason to seek such norms.

Typically (though not always), we are moved to criticize the practice of another community because their practice violates a norm we accept. For purposes of effective cross-cultural social criticism, however, the critic must appeal to norms that will make a difference to people in the community being criticized. There are certain moral precepts that are common to many communities. Prohibitions against such things as murder, deceit, and betrayal are found in many cultures, even in communities with very different social practices. However different human communities may be from one another, we can expect that their institutions and practices will have certain similarities. Human beings are everywhere alike in that they live in communities, use language, and cooperate with one another. Community, language, and cooperative activity are features of every culture, and certain norms are absolutely necessary for such cultural artifacts. Such principles, reiterated across human communities because of certain similarities in their practices, Walzer calls in *Thick and Thin* "minimal morality."

> Minimal morality is very important, both for the sake of criticism and for the sake of solidarity....It consists in principles and rules that are reiterated in different times and places, and that are seen to be similar even though they are expressed in different idioms and reflect different histories and different versions of the world. I won't consider here the reasons for the reiterations or for the differences (a naturalistic account seems best for the first, a cultural account for the second). It is enough to stress the dual effect of these principles and rules. In context, everyday, they provide contrasting perspectives; seen from a distance, in moments of crisis and confrontation, they make for commonality. (Walzer 1994, 16–17)

Minimal morality may offer limited resources for intercultural advocacy of social reform, but it is not the only source of common norms in different communities. Communities commonly adopt one another's practices. In this way, different communities have historically influenced one another. People see the advantages of others' discoveries and inventions and take them over as their own, adapting them to their own needs and circumstances. This is as true in politics and morals as it is in medicine or engineering. The argument from cultural relativism that claims that communities are so different that intercultural criticism, discussion, and agreement are impossible overlooks, among other things, cultural and historical facts (Williams 1985, 158; Moody-Adams 1997, chapters 1 and 2).

"[Relativism] has no bite in the modern world," Martha Nussbaum points out in *Women and Human Development*, a book advocating political and legal reforms pertaining to women in India.

> The ideas of every culture turn up inside every other, through the internet and the media. The ideas of feminism, of democracy, of egalitarian welfarism, are now "inside" every known society. Many

forms of moral relativism, especially those deriving from the cultural anthropology of a previous era, use an unrealistic notion of culture. They imagine homogeneity where there is really diversity, agreement or submission where there is really contestation. My observations about India apply here: there is little that is not "internal" to India, once we get a sufficiently complex idea of its traditions. (Nussbaum 2000, 49)

Certain norms of individual rights and egalitarian political democracy in India, norms more or less similar to our own, contend with a variety of other social, political, and religious norms, and, Nussbaum argues, the former in fact find deep resonance with many Indians. The reformer's problem with those in India who oppose egalitarian political reforms is to find arguments that will make a difference with various sorts of Indian traditionalists. Nussbaum argues in some detail that extending to women certain opportunities enjoyed only by Indian men will greatly enhance women's lives. She argues plausibly that certain capabilities are necessary for flourishing human life generally and should for that reason be equally available to everyone. Nussbaum calls these norms "universal" and claims that they are independent of any "particular metaphysical or teleological view" (2000, 83), but it is not clear whether she means to claim that these are practice-independent ethical norms. What matters for her purposes as an advocate for reform is that these norms have currency with Indians or can be made appealing to them. The claim that these norms are independent of practice is not necessary for her argument.

III

In criticizing the practices of past communities, we need not be concerned that the criticism will make a difference to those we criticize. Advocating social reform of those communities is obviously not the point of criticizing their practices. What, then, is the point of such criticism? Does it matter whether the norms used in such criticism were available in the past? Sometimes, historical understanding requires that we judge past practices by our own standards, if only to contrast our view of a past practice with the view of those who participated in the practice. The differences of perspective revealed by such a contrast sometimes pose a problem for our understanding of the past and of our own practices and norms. We may find it difficult to understand how ancient people thought and acted as they did. At the same time, implicated in such problems may be the difficult and important philosophical question of how it is determined whether norms of another time are the same as or different from ours.

Slavery is a case in point. It is obvious to us that slavery is an abominable practice, yet slavery was (and in some places still is) a common practice. We know perfectly well that the ancient Greeks and Romans did not have our conception of individual rights based on Enlightenment egalitarianism, but it is still difficult for us to understand their apparently uncritical acceptance of slavery. The ancient writings on ethics that so influenced our own ideas contain no effective criticism of slavery as a practice.[1] How could the ancients have been blind to the wrongness of slavery? Is this question naïve and parochial? Or do we think, with good reason, that those who practiced slavery failed to see that slavery was wrong by their own standards—that they should have realized themselves that their practice was bad?

In *Shame and Necessity*, Bernard Williams took these questions very seriously. How far, he asked, does our rejection of slavery depend upon "modern conceptions that were not available in the ancient

---

1. As Paul Veyne noted in *From Pagan Rome to Byzantium*, although ancient Romans disapproved of *individual instances* of extreme cruelty of masters to slaves, they generally did not criticize the practice (1987, 65–67). "No slave, no master, was ever able to imagine a world in which the institution of slavery did not exist" (Veyne 1987, 64).

world?" (1993, 106) He concluded that the ancient Greek acceptance of slavery was not due to a lack of moral conceptions but rather to a conviction that slavery was necessary (1993, 116–17). "The main feature of the Greek attitude to slavery...was not a morally primitive belief in its justice, but the fact that considerations of justice and injustice were immobilized by the demands of what was seen as social and economic necessity. That phenomenon has not so much been eliminated from modern life as shifted to different places" (1993, 125).

It would be hard at any time for those familiar with slavery to miss the fact that the condition of the slave is particularly wretched. To be completely and permanently subordinate to the whim and will of others is a dreadful predicament. The slaves' desires count for practically nothing. The slave, moreover, is vulnerable to any malicious impulse of a master. A slave can be maintained in this unfortunate position only by the threat or use of force. These facts were available to anyone familiar with slavery.

For the masters, to have slaves is to be at war with them (Walzer 1983, 250 n.).

> At any moment, Seneca says, death may catch you unawares: you may fall victim to shipwreck or bandits, "and leaving aside higher powers, the least of your slaves holds over you the power of life and death." A worried Pliny wrote to alert one of his correspondents that his friend Robustus had left on a journey accompanied by some of his slaves and had disappeared. No one had seen him since. "Had he been the victim of an attack by his servants?" In Mainz an epitaph immortalizes the tragic end of a thirty-year-old slaveowner murdered by his slave, who then committed suicide by jumping into the Main. The Romans lived in unspoken fear of their slaves. (Veyne 1987, 51)

Circumstances might from time to time put masters at the mercy of their slaves, but in general, it was the slaves who were particularly vulnerable. From the slaves' perspective, they were, because of the huge disparity of power between themselves and their masters, worse off than combatants in a war. The relationship of masters and slaves has few of the features of community, solidarity, or cooperative practice. Mutuality, trust, and fellow-feeling could exist between master and slave only fleetingly, precariously at the margins of their association.

In his very general criticisms of slavery, published in *The Spirit of the Laws* in 1748, Montesquieu discussed the consequences of the practice of slavery for the participants' characters.

> Slavery, properly so called, is the consequence of establishing the right of one man to own another, to become absolute master over his life and property. There is nothing good about the nature of slavery. It is useful neither to the master nor to the slave. The slave can achieve nothing as the result of being virtuous. As for the master, he acquires all sorts of bad habits from his relationship to his slaves. Without being aware of it, he becomes accustomed to behaving with a total absence of moral virtue; he becomes proud, hasty, severe, irascible, voluptuous, cruel. (Montesquieu 1748, 200–201)

Montesquieu overstated his points—at different times and in various ways, slavery has been useful to individuals and to communities. There have been kind masters and loyal slaves. Slavery, however, puts certain individuals completely at the mercy of others. This sort of complete subordination, as Montesquieu said, breeds cruelty, and so on, on one side, and, he might have added, apathy, deviousness, hatred, and cringing servility, on the other. Such characters are ill suited for a wide range of activities requiring cooperation among people and for social life generally. The types of character the institution tends to promote are bad in any community. Slavery tends to corrupt both master and slave. Modern egalitarian political morality is not required to understand such criticisms.

It is not necessary to possess notions of human rights to see the wretchedness caused by slavery and the deleterious effects of slavery on participants and on community. Williams goes even further: it was widely recognized in ancient Greece that it is a great misfortune to be taken into slavery, "a paradigm of bad luck." The arbitrariness of this calamity was apparent to the Greeks, and they accepted slavery only because they thought it necessary. "No way of life was accessible to [the Greeks] that preserved what was worthwhile to them and did without slavery" (Williams 1993, 111–12). Williams's position is that if the Greeks had raised the question, they could have seen that slavery is unjust. Slavery, though, was necessary for their way of life, or so they thought, and therefore they did not raise the question (Williams 1993, 105–18).[2]

In other words, according to Williams, there is a principle of justice we share with the ancient Greeks according to which slavery is unjust, which principle the Greeks did not apply to slavery because they could not see how they could live without slavery. This is possible. Since we are the cultural heirs of the ancient Greeks, we may have inherited the principle of justice from them. Perhaps a principle that forbids *arbitrarily* depriving individuals of such great goods as freedom is an item of "minimal morality." The *same norm* is to be found with the ancient Greeks as with us. The Greeks simply did not apply the principle to slavery.

An analogy enhances the plausibility of Williams's claims. Consider the case of the Eighth Amendment to the Constitution of the United States. It forbids "cruel and unusual punishments." In 1791, when the amendment was adopted, public flogging was a common punishment. Most of those who voted for the amendment, according to Ronald Dworkin in *Life's Dominion*, did not regard flogging as

2. The historian Paul Veyne claims that slavery was not economically necessary for the ancient Romans, that there were adequate numbers of nonslave laborers for agricultural and domestic tasks (1987, 55).

a cruel punishment (1993, 135–36). Yet today, nearly every American would regard public flogging as paradigmatic of cruel punishment. How could people in the late eighteenth century fail to see the cruelty of flogging? Apparently, what counts as cruelty changed in little more than two hundred years. To say that we are now more sensitive to the suffering of corporal pain simply describes the change, it does not explain it. How could the late eighteenth-century Americans miss the cruelty of flogging? Perhaps they thought that flogging was appropriate because it "fit" certain crimes. Perhaps they thought that it was necessary as a deterrent to certain offenses. Nonetheless, it is presumably *the same constitutional norm* that was adopted in 1791 that we would appeal to now in arguing that flogging is an unconstitutional punishment. Yet that norm has changed in that it is now applied to things that it was not applied to formerly.[3] Williams's position is that a principle by which we find slavery unjust is a principle of justice that had currency in ancient Greece. The Greeks did not find slavery unjust because they did not apply that principle to slavery, just as Americans of the eighteenth century did not apply the Eighth Amendment to flogging. The principle of justice has changed, however, just as the Eighth Amendment has changed. Both norms are now applied to things to which they were not formerly applied.

Williams claimed that slavery is unjust according to an ancient Greek norm of justice, and that if the Greeks had raised the question of the justice of slavery, they might have seen that slavery is unjust. The claim is not obviously true, nor does Williams support it by an account of ancient notions of justice. The Greeks did,

---

3. This is the phenomenon of continuity in change of norms. Recognizing it is the first step in understanding how the interpretation of a norm can change it by applying it in new ways. It is the basis for understanding the difference between interpreting an existing norm and creating a new one, the difference between interpretation and legislation.

however, have a conception of distributive justice. The manner in which people were enslaved in the ancient world could be viewed as an arbitrary deprivation of slaves of the great good of freedom.[4]

Certain norms by which slavery can be judged to be a bad practice did not spring into existence only three hundred years ago, like a theory in a Kuhnian scientific revolution, morally and intellectually discontinuous with everything that had gone before. As one would expect from the influence of the ancient Greeks on us, there is a development from their ideas and practices to ours. There is change in these conceptions, but there is also substantial continuity. How far the acceptance of slavery by the ancients was due to a lack of modern ideas and how far it was due to an unreflective assumption that there was no way to do without slavery is not settled. Perhaps both factors were involved. That misfortune and corrupting influences are bad are matters of minimal morality, norms to be found in some form in any community. The practice of slavery visited terrible misfortune on slaves, and it tended to corrupt both slaves and masters. The precept that it is unjust for individuals or an entire community arbitrarily to deprive individuals of a great good such as freedom may well have had currency in some form with the ancients. If so, they did not apply the norm to slavery. They hardly ever raised the question of the acceptability of slavery as a practice, and this is difficult for us to understand.[5]

---

4. Aristotle discusses distributive justice in *Nicomachean Ethics*, Book V, Chapter 3. For a discussion of Aristotle on slavery, see Williams 1993, 109–16.

5. These and other difficulties in comparing ancient practices with our own will also encumber attempts to decide whether there has been moral progress from ancient times to the present. Not only is it difficult to decide how far our ideas of justice are different from theirs, it will be at least as hard to decide whether and how far ours are better.

FOUR *General and Particular in Practical Knowledge*

Practical knowledge, knowledge of better and worse ways of doing things, arises from people's encounters with the world and their sharing with others what they learn on these occasions. The encounters are particular events, but what is learned is general. What is learned is also normative. The knowledge provides guidance for action and standards for evaluation and criticism. The use of the practical knowledge so acquired is to enable people to cope with the next particular problem—and the next.

If we wish to gain a critical understanding of an existing item of practical knowledge, a norm, then we can look to the particular sorts of problems that called it into existence, and we can examine its use with problems now before us. As with any artifact, the nature of an item of practical knowledge is most fully revealed in its use, and its paradigmatic use will be in a particular case that presents a particular problem.

The relevance of these general observations to ethics will be apparent if ethics is understood as a variety of practical knowledge. Ethics, after all, has to do with our knowledge of better and worse ways of doing things. It is apparent from this perspective that ethical knowledge is general and normative. It is also the case that this knowledge originates in particular encounters and that it is continually revised at the same time that it guides people in their activity on particular occasions. In ethics, as in other kinds of practical knowledge, general and particular are equally important. Ethical knowledge is the result of the continual interplay of general and particular; neither is more fundamental than the other.

When we reflect on solving practical problems, this continual interaction of the particular and the normative general may be rendered obscure because of the persistent influence of a conception of being guided by norms that is obviously mistaken. The conception—"rule formalism"—mistakenly assumes that being guided by norms comes to the same thing as being guided exclusively by what Frederick Will calls the manifest contents of norms.[1] The application of a norm to a particular problem is thus conceived as a matter of matching the explicit content of the norm to the facts of the situation. Should the manifest content of more than one norm match the particular situation, and should the norms indicate contrary courses of action—in other words, should two or more norms conflict—rule formalism confronts a crisis. One obvious response from the rule formalist's perspective is to deny that moral principles ever conflict. So a formalist might hold that there is really only one (fundamental) moral principle. An alternative formalist solution is to maintain that directions for resolving conflicts among multiple principles is built into the manifest content of the principles themselves, one possibility being that there are principles that indicate how to resolve conflicts among principles.

Even when this mistaken conception is recognized as such and rejected (and it is now *widely* rejected), rule formalism continues to exert its influence. Its influence is such that when a philosopher rejects the view, the possibility of a satisfactory account of the guidance of norms seems to be exhausted. Philosophers remain focused exclusively on the manifest content of norms. When rule

1. H. L. A. Hart used the term "formalism" to describe a similar view about legal norms. See his *The Concept of Law* (1961), chapter 7.

formalism is set aside, it appears that, short of giving up the idea that general norms afford rational guidance at all, the only recourse is to a sort of view commonly called "intuitionism." According to this view, one applies norms in hard cases by intuiting their correct application. What intuiting is supposed to be in this regard is not clear, because the rejected conception of the rational guidance of norms, rule formalism, seems to exhaust the possible accounts of this matter. Intuitionism, consequently, is an idea in search of a content—an account of something, I know not what, that enables us intelligently to apply and follow general norms in hard cases.

I

According to rule formalism, the mistaken but influential view, rightness and reasonableness in practical matters have two stages or movements. First we make, discover, or receive general precepts that are the guides and standards of the right or appropriate in activities. These precepts may be in the form of instructions or principles or rules. Next, we compare with our store of general knowledge the features of particular situations in which we seek guidance and do what the precepts indicate for cases having those features. To show that an act is correct or appropriate, we bring the act under a precept; we show that it accords with the rule. If the precept is known to be the right rule, then the matter is settled. A philosopher who subscribes to this view in ethics seeks authoritative precepts that unambiguously indicate the morally appropriate action in every case. The sought-for precepts will be ones that offer a characterization of all and only the situations in which they apply and which correctly tell us what to do in those circumstances. These precepts are the standards of right practical reasoning and moral justification.

According to rule formalism, the proper application of norms is determined by their manifest content alone. Rule formalism fosters a tendency to think of a norm as applying to a situation independently of other norms on the basis of the norm's manifest content alone. Some versions of rule formalism that countenance the possibility of conflicts of norms (and other sorts of problem cases for the application of a norm) allow that there may be one or more rules that explicitly indicate how to apply norms in hard cases—norms for applying norms. When applying a single norm on this view, however, it is not thought necessary to consider the application of an entire body of norms of which the norm is a member. The latent content of norms that belongs to norms as members of bodies of norms is thus rendered invisible. Rule formalism is a form of epistemological atomism with regard to applying and following norms. The idea that rules are applied individually in abstraction from other norms and the idea that their application is determined entirely by the manifest content of norms support one another.

Reasons for acting are sometimes construed on the model of rule formalism. When one cites a reason, on this view, one appeals to an implicit rule. So, if the fact that a man is in a church is a reason for his removing his hat, then there is a rule to the effect that every man in similar circumstances should, or at least has reason to, remove his hat. The implicit rule is conceived as rules are according to rule formalism.

Rule formalism in ethics confronts an initial difficulty: There are not any obvious candidates among familiar moral precepts for rules that fit the requirements of the view. There are, in addition, further problems for the view.

In *The Concept of Law*, Hart offered the following remarks about rule formalism: "Particular fact-situations do not await us already marked off from each other, and labelled as instances of the general rule, the application of which is in question; nor can the rule itself step forward to claim its own instances" (1961, 123). Obviously, we the users must apply the rules, and sometimes their application is problematic. In some situations, it is unclear or controverted whether certain rules apply. It often happens, too, that applicable rules will conflict with one another and indicate contrary courses of action. It is crucial that we apply these rules rightly. How do we do that? The most general version of rule formalism tells us that in order to do something the right way, we must find an authoritative rule that transparently indicates how we correctly perform the task. This will hold for the important task of applying rules.[2] We might seek rules of interpretation to guide us in applying rules to particular cases, but this project encounters daunting difficulties. Where would we find such rules? How would we know when we have the right ones? When the application of a rule of interpretation is problematic in a particular case, what would guide us in applying it correctly? (See Murphy 1964, 116–18; and Wallace 1988, chapter 2.)

Rules, Hart said, cannot "provide for their own interpretation" (1961, 123). If, however, one is drawn to formalism and at the same time struck by the frequency with which the application to practice of rules, precepts, and instructions is problematic, then there appears to be a gap between an important set of situations in which we need guidance in acting and the precepts that we look to for guidance. Because of the nature of the problem, the project of filling the gap with more rules is very unpromising. The predicament of formalism is suggestively similar to that of adherents to Plato's theory of forms confronted with the "Third Man Argument" (Plato, *Parmenides*, 132 a–b; Aristotle, *Metaphysics*, 990b 9–17 and 1059b 8–9).

Rule formalism is so obviously unsatisfactory that one might wonder whether anyone ever held such a view. In fact, the view was common in early modern moral philosophy, where moral principles tended to be conceived on the model of axioms in a deductive system. The influence of the view is apparent in the way philosophers

---

2. For a discussion of rules for applying rules, see J. D. Arras, "Getting Down to Cases: The Revival of Casuistry in Bioethics" (1991), 39–41. This matter is discussed from the perspective of Kant's moral philosophy in O. O'Neill, *Constructions of Reason* (1989), 180–86.

approached the problem of conflicting moral principles. So Immanuel Kant, in the introduction to *The Metaphysics of Morals*, denied the possibility of a conflict of moral norms.

> Since duty and obligation are concepts that express the objective practical *necessity* of certain actions and two rules opposed to each other cannot be necessary at the same time, if it is a duty to act in accordance with one rule, to act in accordance with the opposite rule is not a duty but even contrary to duty; so a *collision of duties* and obligations is inconceivable. (Kant 1797, 16. Emphasis in the original.)

Consider the following passage by John Stuart Mill (*A System of Logic* 1961).

> There must be some standard by which to determine the goodness or badness, absolute and comparative, of ends or objects of desire. And whatever that standard is, there can be but one: for if there were several ultimate principles of conduct, the same conduct might be approved by one of those principles and condemned by another; and there would be needed some more general principle as umpire between them. (Mill 1961, book 6, chapter 12, section 7, 620–21)

Mill used a similar argument in chapter 5 of *Utilitarianism* in his discussion of the adjudication among a plurality of "maxims" of justice (1957). Henry Sidgwick concluded his *Methods of Ethics* on a despairing note because he found that two of his fundamental practical principles appeared to conflict with one another in such a way that they would recommend contrary courses of action in particular cases. Such a "fundamental contradiction," he feared, invited "universal skepticism" about ethics (Sidgwick 1907, 506–9).

In the twentieth century, English-speaking moral philosophers tended to reject rule formalism and adopt an intuitionistic account of how rules are properly applied in hard cases. Certain forms of intuitionism are a response to the perceived failure of rule formalism to account for the practice of applying rules in cases where rules conflict or where their applicability is unclear. W. D. Ross's position in *The Right and the Good* is a classic example (1930, 16–47). More recently, J. O. Urmson has rejected formalism and defended intuitionism.

> If it be recognized that there is a plurality of primary moral reasons for action, the complexity of many situations seems to me to make it implausible to suppose that we are guided (presumably unwittingly) by any decision-procedure when we weigh up pros and cons. I also doubt whether our moral beliefs have the internal harmony requisite for a decision-procedure to be even theoretically possible. This leaves us with the need for an intuitive weighing up of the reasons; since this seems not to be an irrational anomaly but our ordinary predicament with regard to reasons in most fields, I find this conclusion neither surprising nor unduly distressing. (Urmson 1974–75, 119)

John Rawls characterized intuitionism about the application of rules as the alternative to rule formalism. "Intuitionist theories, then, have two features: first, they consist of a plurality of first principles which may conflict to give contrary directives in particular types of cases; and second, they include no explicit method, no priority rules, for weighing these principles against one another: we are simply to strike a balance by intuition, by what seems to us most nearly right" (Rawls 1971, 1999, 30). When considering the possibility that his two fundamental principles of justice might conflict in certain cases, Rawls debated whether to adopt the formalist device of ranking the two principles in the abstract so that the first would have to be satisfied before the second could be applied (appeal to a "priority rule") or to leave the resolution of conflicts between the principles to "intuition." He clearly was not satisfied with either option, but, assuming that these were the only viable options, Rawls chose to rank the two principles as "an illuminating approximation under certain special though significant conditions" (1971, 1999, 36–40). Rawls's uneasy ambivalence about rule formalism and intuitionism is typical.

In *Making Sense of Humanity*, Bernard Williams, following John Rawls's discussion of intuitionism, characterizes a view as "intuitionist if it admits a plurality of first principles that may conflict, and, moreover, it has no explicit method or priority rules for resolving such conflicts" (1995, 182). This characterization means, in effect, that any view of reasonably applying rules that is not a version of rule formalism is intuitionism, and it strongly suggests that intuitionism will be silent about *how* rules are properly applied.

Silence on this point is unsatisfactory. It is crucial that norms be applied in the right way. What, though, is this activity of applying precepts in hard cases? What does one properly do? What are the standards for performing *correctly* the sort of intuitive judging or weighing up of reasons that is not simply a matter of mechanically subsuming particular cases under general precepts?

The last question is obviously crucial. From the formalist perspective, the only way to be guided rightly by a rule is to do what the rule explicitly says in circumstances clearly indicated by the rule itself. In response to the claim that there is also a disciplined activity of applying several rules together in hard cases, an activity that can be done properly and intelligently, the formalist asks how one can show that a rule is applied correctly in a hard case. The formalist might well suspect that what the intuitionist offers as the result of some sort of rational procedure is really a charade culminating in an arbitrary pronouncement.

Indeed, certain intuitionists seem vulnerable on this point. W. D. Ross, in his early and influential rejection of rule formalism, was struck by the multiplicity of irreducibly different ethical considerations that frequently come into conflict with one another in practical problems. He found implausible the idea that there are general principles or algorithms that indicate in every solvable practical problem which of the conflicting considerations properly prevails. Reasonable, well-brought-up individuals, Ross maintained, are able to judge correctly which considerations are stronger in a practical situation. The individual simply sees what the right resolution of the conflicting precepts is. No authoritative general principle can be cited to justify all these judgments, according to Ross, and no fuller account can be given of how such a judgment properly is made (1930, 17–47).

Ross's account positively invites the question, what is the difference between reasonably judging in a practical problem that precept A predominates over precept B and simply opting for A over B for no reason at all? A remark Wittgenstein made in another connection is to the point: "In the present case I have no criterion of correctness. One would like to say: whatever is going to seem right to me is right. And that only means that here we can't talk about 'right'" (1953, 92e).

So compelling is the model of applying rules offered by rule formalism that when philosophers reject the view, as it seems now to most philosophers that they must, there seem to be no alternatives other than intuitionism—which really does not offer an account at all. As long as being guided by norms is conceived as applying single norms to particular cases in isolation from one another, the latent content of norms will be left out of the account, and no good alternative to rule formalism will be visible.

II

A number of contemporary philosophers, taking seriously Rawls's worry that neither rule formalism nor Rossian intuitionism is very satisfactory, attempt to create an alternative third position by the heroic means of giving up on general precepts altogether. They adopt the view that it is the particular judgment rather than the general rule that is normative and guides rational choice. This view, extreme particularism, can be seen as a reaction to the perceived inadequacies of both rule formalism and of its methodological intuitionist alternative. Since it appears that no satisfactory account of how general precepts provide guidance in hard cases is available, this view dispenses with precepts altogether and seeks norms in particular judgments. One simply discerns in the particular case the right thing to do without the need for precepts.

So, Martha Nussbaum rejects the idea that "rational choice can be captured in a system of general rules or principles which can then simply be applied to each new case." She recommends "a defense of the priority of concrete situational judgments of a more informal and intuitive kind to any such system." The "system" referred to here is a "systematic science concerned throughout with universal and general principles" (1990, 66). She cites with approval what she calls "Aristotle's defense of the priority of perception."[3] "Occasion by occasion," John McDowell says in *Mind, Value, and Reality*, "one knows what to do, if one does, not by applying universal principles, but by being a certain kind of person: one who sees situations in a certain distinctive way" (1998, 73). In *Moral Reasons*, Jonathan Dancy says, presumably with McDowell's version of Aristotle in mind: "This virtuous person is not conceived of as someone equipped with a full list of moral principles and an ability correctly to subsume each new case under the right one. There is nothing that one brings to the new situation other than a contentless ability to discern what matters where it matters, an ability whose presence in us is explained by our having undergone a successful moral education" (1993, 50). The difference between these views and Rossian intuitionism comes to this: instead of simply judging that one general precept trumps another in a particular case, there being no general

---

3. For a detailed criticism of this interpretation of Aristotle, see T. H. Irwin, "Ethics as an Inexact Science: Aristotle's Ambitions for Moral Theory," in Hooker and Little 2000, 100–129.

account of why this judgment is right, the extreme particularist view dispenses altogether with the need for general precepts and asserts that one directly perceives or discerns the right course of action in the case. Besides denying, contrary to all appearances, that practical norms (and the knowledge they embody) are general, extreme particularism appears to embrace the difficulties of intuitionism. Nussbaum sees an important role for general rules:

> They might be used not as normative for perception, the ultimate authorities against which the correctness of particular choices is assessed, but more as summaries or rules of thumb, highly useful for a variety of purposes, but valid only to the extent to which they correctly describe good concrete judgments, and to be assessed, ultimately, against these. (Nussbaum 1990, 68)

This view suggests that judgments about what should be done in particular situations are in a way like judgments about the colors of particular objects. People learn to make perceptual judgments in a few particular cases and thereby acquire a skill to go on to new cases, without needing generalizations to guide or to justify their subsequent judgments. Thus, a child learns to sort toys by colors and thereby acquires without further tuition the ability to go on to recognize those colors and even novel shades of those colors in a variety of other things. It is possible for people to generalize— grass is generally green, ravens black, and so on—but such general judgments depend ultimately upon the ability to recognize colors in particular cases.

Judgments about right and wrong, however, are often controversial in ways that color judgments are not; the former require justification in ways that judgments about the colors one sees do not. Insofar as particularism claims that we "just see" what should be done in a particular situation, no account being possible about why it is right, the view is vulnerable to the same objections as Rossian intuitionism. In denying that norms are general, moreover, the view is in conflict with much of the apparent phenomena surrounding practical reasoning and criticism.

Nussbaum suggests still another analogy. The ability to make right ethical choices is in a way like the ability to tell jokes or the ability to improvise in music (1990, 94). It is possible to generalize about such things, but the generalizations are dependent upon the ability to make pertinent judgments in particular cases. Thus, it is claimed, in practical reasoning the particular is prior to the general, and it is the particular judgment that is the norm.

III

The ability to sort things by colors, to tell jokes, and to improvise in music are examples of one kind of know-how or practical knowledge. How are we to conceive of the practical knowledge that guides us in such activities? Is it true that what is normative in these cases is particular rather than general? Should we conceive of the ethical knowledge that enables us to judge that particular acts are right or wrong on the model of such discriminatory abilities?

Practical knowledge, know-how, is knowledge of how things are properly done. What we know, items of practical knowledge, are properly called norms. We can sometimes exemplify such norms by acting in ways that express our knowledge—"here is the way to do it." The example is a particular act, but it is meant to exemplify something general—a right way of doing something *in a certain kind of activity*.[4] What one knows in knowing how to sort things by colors or how to tell jokes is general in the sense that it is knowing how to do a certain kind of thing. What is difficult (or perhaps

---

4. Nelson Goodman introduced the topic of exemplification into the philosophy of art in *Languages of Art* (1968, 52–57). For an illuminating discussion of the role of exemplification in understanding, see Catherine Z. Elgin, "Understanding Art and Science" (1991).

impossible) is to formulate this knowledge in a general precept. With other sorts of practical knowledge, however, it is possible to *formulate* in words—as a general instruction, a precept, or a rule—the norm that is exemplified by an action. Such precepts and such exemplifications can be used in teaching norms, in instruction in practical matters. The whole purpose of such instruction is to communicate something general—the instructor's point is not just to show students how to treat *this* wound, but how to treat wounds *of this kind.* By means of examples and precepts, people are able to benefit from the practical experience of others and acquire the general knowledge of how to do something. This general knowledge is a guide; it is normative. There are particular imperatives, as when the sergeant says to the private, "Take this message to headquarters." By contrast, "Keep your weapon clean and oiled" is a general precept of soldiering. We have a good idea of the particular experiences that have given rise to this precept.

Norms, standards of right and wrong, are by their very nature general, although they are expressed and communicated by particular examples or by particular formulations. Thus, the formalists and Rossian intuitionists are right in a way about the generality of norms. To avoid the weaknesses of their views, however, it is crucial that norms, their exemplifications by actions, and their formulations in precepts be understood in a certain way. Norms must be thought of as "social-psychological entities," shared "habits," components of learned activities that comprise many norms in a structure that relates the norms to one another. In our activities, we encounter norms not individually but in collections, in "corporate bodies" that make up the activities. A norm guides our activity, not as an isolated item, but in concert with many other norms. Soldiers know that there are situations in which other matters properly take precedence over cleaning a weapon because they know how to follow the precept "Keep your rifle clean and oiled" together with the other precepts comprised by soldiering. Those who have mastered an activity such as soldiering do not have a set of precepts that tell them unambiguously and explicitly what to do in every case they encounter. Instead, they know how to soldier. Much of what they know can be formulated as precepts, instructions.

Frederick Will's distinction between the manifest and the latent aspects of norms is useful in this connection (1997, 163–66; 1988, 147–52). The manifest aspect of a norm of automobile driving in a certain jurisdiction might be captured in the formulation of an instruction to keep to the right except to pass. A driving instructor might issue such an instruction to students. Driving students who take this to mean that they are to keep to the right unless passing another vehicle *no matter what* imperfectly understand the instruction. The norm is only one among a great many other norms that together regulate and guide the activity of automobile driving. To understand the instruction to drive to the right, one must understand how this norm functions in concert with other norms that the activity of driving comprises—one must understand the precept's latent content, in addition to its manifest content. Such understanding includes, among a great many other things, grasping the point of keeping traffic moving in the same direction to the same side of the road, together with such things as appreciating the necessity of avoiding obstacles in a driver's path and the necessity of moving to the left in order to make a left turn.

The precept that one should return a borrowed item to its owner when the owner asks for it *says* that one should return the object on the owner's demand. Someone who supposes that this means that one should return a borrowed weapon when its berserk owner demands it imperfectly understands the precept. There is not necessarily anything wrong with formulating the precept with the words, "One should return a borrowed object when its owner asks for it." When the madman asks for his hand grenade, of course, one will not give it to him. This particular practical judgment normally will not take much thought at all. The judgment is not, however, simply the exercise of a "contentless ability," nor is it an ineffable intuition about the applicability of a principle. A relatively articulate practitioner can explain cogently, albeit tediously, why, despite the importance of returning borrowed items across a wide range of practice, concerns with protecting the deranged owner and innocent bystanders are relevant, too. Property is important, and so is the fact that the borrower has the property on trust, but these are parts of a corporate body of norms that includes, among a great many other things, protecting the mentally infirm and preventing serious harm to others. A person's property rights do not generally include the liberty to use the property to injure people. Such general knowledge is part of the latent content of the norm about returning borrowed items. It comes from the body of norms that one confronts when considering whether to return the borrowed object.

Such considerations, including the norms of one or more practices, belong to the latent aspect of the norm formulated by the words, "Keep right except to pass" or "Return borrowed items when the owner demands them." Merely understanding the words that formulate these norms is not sufficient for understanding the norm. This is not to say that there is anything wrong with formulating the norm in this way. If one tries to include the latent content of such norms in their formulation, one will have to formulate the practical knowledge of one who knows how to drive; and this will not be all, since automobile driving is a part of a great many other activities. Similarly, norms dealing with property belong to a wide range of practices. It is not only the sheer amount and complexity of this practical knowledge that makes it infeasible to try to exhaust the latent content of a norm in an explicit formulation. Norms remain open to alteration in the light of unprecedented situations, and their latent content can provide guidance in reforming norms to deal with novel problems. It is not possible to anticipate all unprecedented problems, and so it is not possible to describe in advance how the latent content of norms will be used to adapt a practice to novel problems.

IV

In *Ethics without Principles*, Jonathan Dancy argues that practical reasons function "holistically"—what is a reason for acting in a certain way in one case may not be a reason for so acting in another case—it may even in another case be a reason for doing the opposite. Its being a reason in a particular case depends upon the particulars of the case. "That there will be nobody much else around is sometimes a good reason for going there, and sometimes a very good reason for staying away" (Dancy 2004, 74). "It cannot hold generally, then, that whenever there is nobody around, there is good reason to go there. If reasons function holistically, then we cannot expect there to be truths of the form, 'Whenever features a, b, and c are present, there is a reason to do x.'" That (most) moral reasons function holistically, Dancy claims, rules out the possibility that there can be a comprehensive ethics of principle (2004, 73–77). What holism rules out, I think, is the possibility of moral reasons and principles *as rule formalism would have us conceive them*.

Formalists seek rules that unambiguously indicate what is to be done. Yet in the realm of practice rules too often fail to provide guidance, when guidance is so conceived. Despite the extreme particularists, we do apply rules in hard cases, so, it is assumed, there must be *something* that *unambiguously* indicates how to proceed with the rules. This something is the method of intuitionism, but what this is is elusive and obscure. A part of the reason for its elusiveness is that there is generally nothing that indicates *unambiguously* how to apply rules in hard cases. The sort of guidance provided by the latent aspect of norms is not of this sort.

Dewey's slogan that principles should be thought of as instruments is useful here. Don't think of a precept as simply a grammatical sentence that interacts formally with other sentences. Think of it as a tool that has proved useful with certain tasks, that may be used with new tasks, although perhaps only with some improvisation and additional cost. Dewey also helpfully recommends that we think of precepts as hypotheses—generalizations that have proved useful but remain open to modification in the light of further experience. He said, too, that practical principles are the intellectual counterparts of "habits"—that is, they are formulations of norms that are tendencies to act. All these metaphors are useful in resisting the powerful pull of the conception of norms in rule formalism. It is important to take seriously the fact that precepts formulate elements of living practices.

A bit of imagined medical history may serve to illustrate these points. A proto-physician has learned to treat broken limbs by splinting them—experience has shown that a splinted break heals better. The physician then encounters a patient with broken ribs or a broken collarbone. What from the relatively successful treatment for broken arms and legs can be adapted to a case of broken bones that cannot be splinted? The physician might recall that tightly wrapping a broken water vessel held the pieces together rigidly enough to permit the pot to be usable. The wrapping held the edges of the broken pieces rigidly together in a way somewhat like the way the broken pieces of a leg bone are held together by a splint. This *suggests* tightly wrapping the torso of a patient with broken ribs. Nothing unambiguously indicates that since a broken pot is like a human torso with broken ribs in certain ways, broken ribs can be repaired in the way pots are repaired. The similarities suggest trying something.

This imaginary piece of reasoning shows how general knowledge derived partly from past experience in a practical area relatively remote from medicine might be used, adapted, to solve a problem novel in an individual's experience. What could emerge from this solution, assuming that it works, is a notion of immobilizing and holding together pieces of broken bones, including splinting where feasible, but now including another way of immobilizing. This is an altered norm, realized by using the latent aspect of norms of healing and norms from another area of practice.

The sort of particularism in ethics that is indicated by these reflections is not one that dispenses with the general in deciding what to do in hard cases. The particular case can and often does present a distinctive juxtaposition of general norms. The particular case is crucial because it can determine what general considerations are relevant. To resolve the problem posed, it is necessary to attend to the "distinctive complication" of norms and purposes "which can never repeat itself" (Dewey 1922, 146). The aim in deliberation is properly to devise a way of acting that will enable one as far as possible to accept the guidance of all the competing general norms while being faithful to their latent content, including their purposes, their meanings. The procedure here can be creative and improvisational. There is not *a method* for doing this, nor are there fixed "priority rules." Insofar as calling this process "intuition" suggests that it is not possible to give an account, a rationale for such a deliberation, however, the label is misleading.

V

The extreme particularist in ethics, though, can be understood as claiming that ethical choice is more like telling jokes or distinguishing false from genuine expressions of feeling than driving an automobile or treating broken bones. The practical knowledge of the witty person, even though it is an ability to do a certain *kind* of thing—general knowledge—does not lend itself much to formulation in words as precepts. Making ethical choices, too, the claim continues, is not an activity that lends itself to formulable precepts or instructions. Just as the witty person can repeatedly and successfully tell jokes without being able to formulate precepts that guide the activity, the ethical chooser proceeds without precepts.

The practical knowledge, the norms, involved in various activities, however, does not fall neatly into the formulable and the nonformulable. Wittgenstein says of expertise in judging the genuineness of expressions of feeling:

> Can one learn this knowledge? Yes; some can. Not, however, by taking a course in it, but through *"experience"*. —Can someone else be a man's teacher in this? Certainly. From time to time he gives him the right *tip.* —This is what 'learning' and 'teaching' are like here. —What one acquires here is not a technique; one learns correct judgments. There are also rules, but they do not form a system, and only experienced people can apply them right. Unlike calculation rules.
>
> What is most difficult here is to put this indefiniteness, correctly and unfalsified, into words. (Wittgenstein 1953, 227e. Emphasis in the original.)[5]

Some sorts of practical knowledge lend themselves more readily to formulation in precepts than others. The issue becomes, how far does the practical knowledge involved in ethical choices lend itself to formulation? Since such choices are made across the whole range of human activity, we should expect that the answer for any such choice will depend partly on what the chooser is doing, what the occasion for the choice is, and what matters are at stake in the choice. In other words, it depends on the particular choice. Still, whereas there are no general precepts for the routine discrimination of colors, and few if any precepts for being witty, there are many ethical precepts. The facts are suggestive.

Martha Nussbaum begins the introductory chapter of her book *Love's Knowledge* with the observation that conventional philosophical prose cannot always "fully and adequately" state certain "views of the world and how we should live in it" (1990, 3). If one wants to express the world's variety, complexity, and mysteriousness, she

---

5. Nussbaum quotes the last few lines of this passage as an epigraph at the beginning of chapter 2 of *Love's Knowledge* (1990).

suggests, one does better to use a form of expression that is "more complex, more allusive, more attentive to particulars." The language and forms of the narrative novel are well suited to this purpose. Human acts and choices are frequently the subject of narrative fiction, and Nussbaum chooses novels to exemplify what she calls "the priority of the particular" in ethical reasoning.

In two chapters, Nussbaum (1990, chapters 4 and 5) confronts philosophical accounts of deliberation and choice with a fictional decision of Maggie Verver as it is presented by Henry James in *The Golden Bowl.* The novel, as Nussbaum interprets it, describes a young woman's passage from a less to a more mature, complex, and adequate understanding of ethical choice as it pertains to her situation. Nussbaum uses the novel, so interpreted, to recommend that philosophers, too, move in their conceptions to this more adequate understanding. The contrast that Nussbaum exhibits—between the mechanical, hard-edge, brain-spun contrivance of the formalist thinker, on one hand, and the master novelist's evocation of the rich complexity of ethical choice in real life, on the other—is arresting.

Maggie Verver and her father are wealthy, cultured Americans living in England early in the twentieth century. Maggie discovered that her husband, Amerigo, an impecunious Italian prince, was having a love affair with her friend Charlotte, the young wife of Maggie's father. Maggie's problem was what to do about this discovery. She decided to preserve her own marriage and her father's marriage, while giving up her close and constant companionship with her father. Nussbaum, and presumably James, regard Maggie as choosing well in this. Why was this choice better than the alternatives? Why, for example, should Maggie not have made the continuation of her close, affectionate companionship with her father the predominant consideration, giving up her marriage? How does Maggie's deliberation instance reasonable deliberation and choice, according to Nussbaum?

In "Flawed Crystals" (1990, chapter 4) Nussbaum points out that Maggie's choice reflects "intuitive perception" of all the complex particulars pertaining to her situation and that it reflects Maggie's realization that she cannot have all the things that she had hitherto tried to combine in her life. This realization, Nussbaum says, is part of Maggie's ethical development: in the novel Maggie moves away from the idea that other people's lives can, without significant conflict, be rearranged around hers to suit her high-minded purposes. Maggie wanted the prince and married him. The realization that this left her widowed father with less of her company than formerly prompted Maggie, the loving dutiful daughter, to promote his marriage to her friend Charlotte Stant. Maggie continued after these marriages, however, to spend so much time with her father that her acquaintances regarded the situation as peculiar. The Ververs are highly moralistic; Maggie is bent upon fulfilling all her obligations and hurting no one. The cracked golden bowl in the novel symbolizes the point that the possibility of such perfection is illusory. Maggie learns that "the world of *The Golden Bowl* is a fallen world" (Nussbaum 1990, 133). To live as a married woman with her husband, she must give up altogether her role as companion to her father, and she must hurt her friend Charlotte. In this way, Nussbaum uses the novel to focus our attention on the necessity of accepting the inevitability of the conflict of goods and duties in an individual's life.

Maggie's choice and Nussbaum's interpretive comments provide an unusually fecund example of deliberation and choice for philosophical purposes. What shows, though, that Maggie's choice of what to preserve and what to give up is a good one? Nussbaum tells us that deliberation is properly a matter of "intuitive perception and improvisatory response," and this is how Maggie proceeded (1990, 134–38, 141). Maggie rightly abandons the immature idea that it is always possible to lead a life in which one is able successfully to pursue all important goods and fulfill all obligations. Nussbaum says plausibly that Maggie replaced this idea with the understanding that life requires one to make painful choices, to give things up in order to have other things. Maggie learned that she must hurt others, leave certain obligations unfulfilled, in order to fulfill other ones. Living one's life as one should is not well conceived as simply fitting together everything desirable and everything one is committed to. Life inevitably forces choices that require us to accept less than an ideal of completeness and perfection.

Nussbaum explicitly adopts "the very simple Aristotelian idea that ethics is the search for the specification of the good life for a human being" (1990, 139). Yet she notes with approval Maggie's ethical epiphany that the good life—the life that is perfect and lacking in nothing that would make it better—is unrealizable, that one is forced to choose something that falls short of such a life. The "very simple Aristotelian ideal," if it is taken to be the proper aim of ethical choice, is perilously close to the view that Maggie abandons, the ethically immature view. The fallback position, that although the perfect life is unrealizable, one properly aims in one's decisions to come as close to it as possible, is tempting at this point. Which of the indefinitely many ways of winnowing and fitting together various goods in a human life, though, is perfect? Even if we could discover a plausible answer to this question, how would we determine which of several alternative particular lives comes closest to the ideal one? How are we to judge closeness? Even if there were such a thing as *the* good human life, a description of it is of dubious relevance when we face choices like Maggie's. Knowledge of how to play the perfect bridge hand is not likely to help one to know how to play the hand one is dealt.

Why was Maggie's decision in response to her discovery of the relationship between her husband and Charlotte a good one? It is important that she was scrupulously attentive to the particulars of her situation, but this is not sufficient for choosing rightly. It is important that she abandoned the infeasible idea that that she could retain everything—her close companionship with her father, her marriage, her friendship with Charlotte—fulfill her obligations, and avoid hurting anyone. Why, though, was she right in deciding to preserve her marriage and her father's marriage, causing pain to Charlotte and giving up her companionship with her father? She might instead have chosen to retain her position as her father's constant companion, letting the marriages wither. What is needed here is an account of why in the circumstances it was better to give up one thing rather than the other.

In the essay "'Finely Aware and Richly Responsible': Literature and the Moral Imagination," Nussbaum explores Maggie Verver's choice further and develops the idea of "perception" in ethical choice by discussing what she calls "moral imagination" (1990, chapter 5). The discussion focuses upon a single episode in *The Golden Bowl* in which Maggie and her father decide to part, she to stay in England with Amerigo and he to return to America with Charlotte. Nussbaum draws our attention to the imaginative understanding of both daughter and father of each other's situation and the subtlety and delicacy with which each responds to the situation (1990, 149–51).

Maggie and Adam Verver are alone in a garden, and the reference to the Garden of Eden reverberates through the episode. If one were to try to formulate a rationale for the choice that they make, it seems to me that a clue is to be found in the fact that while he is Adam, she is not Eve. Maggie is the daughter, and that makes a great difference. One thing that is represented in this passage, I think, is a scene that is played out between parents and children over and over, sometimes, as in this instance, with great poignancy. Maggie, Nussbaum says, "imaginatively perceives" her father as, in James's words, "a high little man." She understands that she must let him go "as a man, not a failure, with his dignity intact" (1990, 149–50). At the same time, Nussbaum points out, James represents Adam as perceiving Maggie in a certain way, as a sort of sea creature—safe, independent, reveling in the joy of life. Adam sees his daughter clearly as a mature, independent woman, no longer a child in any sense. This perception, which apparently Maggie has contrived with great subtlety and tact to produce, is necessary for Adam's accepting the proposal that they part, he returning to America with his wife and Maggie remaining in England with Amerigo. Adam, unaware of the affair, nonetheless understands that Maggie desires to separate from him, and he understands the importance of communicating to Maggie that he regards such a separation as appropriate in view of her maturity. These realizations by Maggie and her father, and their perceptions of one another, instance what Nussbaum calls moral imagination.

The imaginative perceptions of these two characters are crucial in their decision, but this is compatible with norms, general in character, guiding their choice. Family life is guided by a complex, moving body of practical knowledge. An important element in the decision that Maggie and Adam separate is found in the relationship of parent and child. These ethical roles, based in large part upon the need of human children for prolonged nurture and education, are shaped by the needs that call them forth but also by the complex social life in which they are situated. The relationship of parent and child should be one of love and friendship for each another, though of a form determined partly by the nature of the relationship. Mutual affection adds a particularly desirable dimension to the relationship, supporting the dependent child's feeling protected and important, motivating the parent's constant care. Given the purpose of the relationship—the eventual maturity and independence of the child—the relationship should change, should become less close when the child reaches maturity.

Parents tend to view their children as needing guidance and protection; children view their parents as counselors and protectors. It takes effort for a daughter to see her father as just another man, let alone seeing him lovingly as "a high little man." Similarly, it takes something akin to imagination for a father to see his young adult daughter as a mature woman. Yet this marks the successful completion of the relationship of dependent child and parent. The general point about the appropriateness of a drawing apart of father and mature daughter plays a central role in their reaching their decision. In the case of Adam and Maggie, the close relationship had been unusually prolonged, in part because Maggie was providing companionship for her widowed father. When they decide to part, however, Maggie is married and her widowed father is remarried. Their friends rightly saw the constant companionship of the Ververs as peculiar. Their drawing apart is appropriate. Adam's painful renunciation of the companionship of his daughter, the amputation of what has been a central element in his life, has a certain dignity, even though it comes late. The perception of the daughter as mature and the perception of the father as a limited man have the practical significance they do in this situation because of the norms of family and marriage.

The claim for the *priority* of particular perceptions over general norms is not supported by this example. Nussbaum claims that Maggie's and Adam's perceptions are "prior" to general precepts in that (1) it would not be possible for them to know what principles applied without the particular perceptions, and (2) even if the principles could be applied without the particular perceptions, the application could easily lead to wrong actions (1990, 156). She could have made an equally strong case, however, that general norms are prior to the perceptions—without the norms, the practical significance of the particular perceptions is lost. She offers a better characterization of the roles of particular perceptions and general norms in choice when she describes the novelist as setting in dialogue "perception and rule" (1990, 157–61). The novel "situates rules in their appropriate place vis-à-vis perceptions," she says, inasmuch as "correct judgment is the outcome of a dialogue between antecedent principle and new vision" (160). It is a feature of a dialogue that we know what the parties say, how they interact. In the interaction of general and particular in Maggie's choice, we can say what part each plays. Neither is prior to the other. There is nothing ineffable, no consultation with unformulable intuition.

Much more needs to be said to complete the rationale for the course of action Maggie chose over alternatives that her circumstances allowed. Maggie has a husband whom she loves deeply enough for her affection to survive the discovery of his unfaithfulness. She had in a way failed in a responsibility to her husband. She had hitherto invested in her father the time and emotional capital that would more appropriately go to her spouse. Maggie and Amerigo have a child. The alternative that would enable Maggie and her father to continue their constant companionship would require her, in a sense, to continue to prolong her minority beyond its term, it would constitute continued neglect of her marriage, and it would require her to live with the continuing relationship of her husband and Charlotte. The situation, moreover, is unstable. Should Adam discover the affair, he would be deeply hurt. Their social world would not accept the dissolution of the two marriages and the recombination of the parties. Charlotte and the prince, moreover, have no money. Wealth is a requirement for the lives that the four principals live. Maggie has reason to think that her husband loves her and wants the marriage to continue. There is a case here for the decision that Maggie and Adam made, and the case is made up in equal parts of particular perceptions and general practical knowledge.

The norms in the complex that guided the choice of Maggie and Adam are general ones that pertain to the relationships of friends, parents and children, and husbands and wives. The particular perceptions of the parties are central to their understanding what norms are involved, how their situation juxtaposes these norms, and what responses their circumstances permit. These relationships are rich with general ethical norms, replete with responsibilities and nuanced feelings. The explicit formulations of all the general norms and their juxtaposition in the particular circumstances do not unambiguously indicate that Maggie should have decided as she did. Indeed, the manifest content of these norms points in more than one direction. It is the perceptions, together with practical knowledge consisting of general norms, that together guide the decision and provide the basis for assessing the decision. Maggie opted for maturity, independence, protection of her father's feelings, a troubled marriage with a man she loved, and responsibilities to her child, giving up the close company of her father and her friend, Charlotte. She opted to preserve her father's marriage and dignity, while depriving him of his closest companion. She separated Charlotte and the prince. Nothing guarantees that this will work as she hopes. Many practical choices, including ethical ones, culminate in a course of action to be *tried*. Only the result of the actual trial can conclusively establish that the reasoning was successful, and *The Golden Bowl* ends before these matters have a chance to play themselves out. Just as the proto-physician could discover only by the trial whether a method of repairing pottery could be successfully adapted to treating broken ribs, the success of Maggie's choice depends on what happens when the couples separate and go their different ways. This aspect of practical reasoning accounts for the openness of the indications of pertinent norms. The point here is not that all rules are merely suggestions. The point is that when the problem is that norms are truly hard to apply in a particular circumstance, the reasonable thing to expect from one's practical knowledge is solutions to be tried that are more rather than less likely to work.

The idea that moral precepts are in this sense open and mutable, and that moral reasoning properly can be improvisational, may seem at odds with the "hardness" of the moral ought, with the idea that moral precepts are commands. It is not incompatible with the importance and urgency of moral requirements, however, to accept the idea that when two or more such important precepts conflict in a particular situation, the alternative to adjustment is paralysis. As most of us learn fairly early, moral absolutism, the idea that moral principles are immutable commands, is, in this complex changing world, unsatisfactory, superficial.

Is this account of how instructions, precepts, and rules guide actions in hard cases a form of intuitionism? As Rawls and Williams define the term, any account of how norms guide actions that is not a version of formalism is intuitionism. That is, any view that countenances anything beyond the manifest content of norms as contributing to the rational guidance of conduct by norms is a version of intuitionism. In this sense, I am defending a version of intuitionism. In the current philosophical use of the term, however, intuitionism has the further connotation that no positive account can be given of how precepts are properly applied in cases in which their manifest content is not sufficient for their application—one just "sees" or "judges" that a rule applies or that a rule trumps another applicable rule that conflicts with it. As Rawls put it at one point, "[According to intuitionism] we must eventually reach a plurality of first principles in regard to which we can only say that it seems to us more correct to balance them this way rather than that" (1971, 1999, 34). In this respect, the account I defend is not intuitionistic.

There is not *a method* for applying rules in hard cases, but this is because the actual practical problems that qualify as hard cases are so various and because the better solutions to such problems often require improvisation. There is no method in the sense of an algorithm or a rule of interpretation. A good solution to such a problem, however, is one that takes account, as far as the situation allows, of what is at stake in all the considerations implicated in the problem. This is a paraphrase of Dewey's account of a reasonable choice—a choice that involves "unifying, harmonizing, different competing tendencies," that fulfills them all "not indeed, in their original form, but in a 'sublimated' fashion, that is in a way which modifies the original direction of each by reducing it to a component along with others in an action of transformed quality" (Dewey 1922, 135). This account is abstract, very general. We are not given a definition of what counts as unity and harmony. Norms, however, are a motley, and their possible different juxtapositions in particular situations are uncountable. The aim in general of deliberation can be adequately described only in a general way. With respect to particular practical problems, however, it is often possible to be specific about what the better solution is and why. One is not reduced to saying merely, "It just seems to me that such and such is right." In this respect, possessing a sense of humor is not a good model for practical reasonableness. Insofar as intuitionism implies that one cannot give a general account of how norms can be guides in hard cases or that one cannot explain why a choice such as Maggie Verver's is a good one, intuitionism is mistaken.

FIVE *Virtues of Benevolence and Justice*

> Justice, rigorous justice, is for some people an absolute value, but
> it is not compatible with what may be no less ultimate values for
> them—mercy, compassion—as arises in concrete cases.
> (Berlin 1992, 12)

> We cannot disentangle genuine possession of kindness from
> the sensitivity that constitutes fairness. And since there are
> obviously no limits on the possibilities for compresence,
> in the same situation, of circumstances of the sorts proper
> sensitivities to which constitute all the virtues, the argument
> can be generalized: no one virtue can be fully possessed except
> by a possessor of all of them, that is, a possessor of virtue in
> general.
> (McDowell 1998, 53)

> Character is the interpenetration of habits.
> (Dewey 1922, 29)

Among the norms that constitute practices, I have maintained, are
ethical norms. The ethical norms are components of practices, standards of acting that are exemplified in better rather than worse ways
of doing things. A good person, though, is not merely someone
who is concerned to do things correctly. Kindness, sympathy, and
compassion invariably appear on contemporary lists of ethical virtues, and these traits consist in more than a concern to do things
the right way. How are we to understand the relationship between

ethical norms that are components of practices and such ethical phenomena as "other-regarding" virtues?

People are moved to act by a concern for the welfare of others. Sometimes this concern flows from deep affection for another, as with lovers, friends, and family members. People care also, however, about others whom they know only slightly or not at all. They feel sympathy sometimes for the suffering and misfortune of casual acquaintances and strangers and are moved to aid and comfort them. The special character of this concern for others that all these phenomena exemplify is captured by Aristotle's description in the *Nicomachean Ethics* of the attitude of friends toward one another. "The decent person…is related to his friend as he is to himself, since the friend is another himself" (1166a 30–31, 1999, 142). That is, sympathetic people tend in their feelings and actions to respond to others' fortunes as they do toward their own. This attitude exemplifies the central phenomenon of benevolence; there are, of course, variants and peripheral cases (Brandt 1976, 430–33; Sidgwick 1907, 238–63).

People are also influenced in their actions by a desire to get something right according to a certain standard or norm. Their concern in such actions may be the necessity of observing the norm in order to produce a certain desired result, as when surgeons perform prescribed scrubbing routines to promote antisepsis. Architects, scholars, musicians, and many other kinds of practitioners, however, when they are engaged in complex activities that they value, are sometimes concerned simply to do things right. Their love of the activity, their appreciation of it, is expressed in their concern to do it in accordance with the highest standards they know. When they practice well, their satisfaction is a good that is internal to the practice—it is a good available only to practitioners (MacIntyre 1984, 188–91). The phenomenon of being guided by norms extends to all areas of human life, embracing a wide variety of activities and concerns. Being guided by moral norms is an instance of this general phenomenon.

Kindness, generosity, sympathy, and compassion are prominent virtues of character that are forms of benevolence. At the core of such virtues is a concern for the welfare of others. Honesty, truthfulness, being a person of one's word, and fairness, in contrast, are among the virtues of character that evince a commitment to certain norms of social ethics. For convenience, let us call these, and conscientiousness about ethical norms generally, forms of justice. A just person, then, is a person who possesses these virtues of justice. It is widely thought that to be a person of good character, it is necessary to possess both kinds of virtues—benevolence and justice. It is not always easy, however, to combine these qualities in a single character. Sometimes, one cannot avoid hurting someone without failing in some important obligation. Such situations can be painful for people who are both conscientious and sympathetic. The conflict is a common one in many areas of life; judges, loan officers, members of university tenure committees, teachers, and many others are painfully familiar with it. Such conflict led Isaiah Berlin to say, "Justice, rigorous justice, is for some people an absolute value, but it is not compatible with what may be no less ultimate values for them—mercy, compassion—as arises in concrete cases" (1992, 12).

Consider the tenderhearted teachers. They do not give students failing grades for truly poor work; they don't want to hurt the students' feelings. Giving these students passing grades, however, is bad pedagogical practice. It is, moreover, unfair to better students and to those who rely on accurate evaluations of students' work for important decisions. It can deceive students about the quality of their own work. Many tenderhearted teachers know this, but they cannot bring themselves to hurt and disappoint weak students. Their sympathy leads them to act contrary to pedagogical and ethical norms. They fail the practice they are engaged in by insufficient commitment to its norms. They are deficient in justice. They are too kind.

From the opposite perspective, teachers who grade students' work solely on the basis of the quality of the work, undeterred by the knowledge that some students will as a result be deeply disappointed, even wounded, are just, but they are not necessarily deficient in kindness. There are several possibilities here. A teacher might think that the harm done by misleading a student is greater than the harm of hurt feelings—that it is really no kindness to the students to give them inflated grades. It may be in some cases, though, that a teacher would give the appropriate grade whether or not doing so is in the student's best interest. Here, it appears, the fact that an act that hurts someone is required by a relevant norm can turn aside the charge that in hurting someone, the agent was being unkind. This point suggests that Berlin's claim that justice and compassion are incompatible is an oversimplification.

Immanuel Kant noted that sympathy and benevolence sometimes lead people to act contrary to a moral norm, and thus to act wrongly. Benevolence, therefore, he said, is not good "without qualification." The firm determination to act in accordance with moral norms, however, the trait of character that Kant called "a good will," is sufficient to motivate people to do what they think they should do (1785, 61–71). Benevolence can motivate people to act contrary to norms, including moral norms, whereas the conscientious determination to be guided by a certain moral norm (Kant thought there is only one moral norm) is not an incentive to violate the norm. It would seem to follow, then, that moral character is simply a matter of commitment to the relevant norms. Benevolence is, at best, an unreliable ally of Kantian good will. Kant did not draw the conclusion that benevolence is a dispensable element in good character, although his view of benevolence was ambivalent. (For a discussion of the vexed question of Kant's view of the place of benevolence in good character, see Baron 1995, 207–26.)

John McDowell, in contrast, holds that to be a genuinely kind person, one must also possess all the other virtues (1998, 53). He is led to this view because he regards all the virtues as matters of knowing and doing what one should do in particular circumstances.

McDowell wants to replace ethical norms as guides to right actions with virtues that will in every case lead a person to do what is right. So one who acts wrongly out of a direct concern for another's welfare contrary to the requirements of fairness could not on McDowell's view be expressing the virtue genuine kindness. By contrast, although Kant accepts for the virtue good will this model of a virtue as a matter of knowing and doing what one should do, he conceives benevolence in a different way. It is not necessary to embrace Kant's conception of freedom of the will in order to agree with him that benevolence is a direct concern for the welfare of others that can occasion conflict with a commitment to norms.

It is a central tenet of at least some versions of "virtue ethics" that any and all of the ethical virtues are dispositions to know the right thing to do and to do it. (In addition to McDowell, see Hursthouse 1999, 8–16.) The traits that philosophers, both ancient and modern, regard as ethical virtues, however, are a motley. They differ too much from one another to fit such generalizations as the tenet. Courage and virtues of benevolence are among virtues that do not fit the tenet. (For further discussion of this point, see Jacobson 2005.)

Someone might not be benevolent and still be brave and honest. We think, nevertheless, that a person should have the virtues of benevolence. The view that a person might altogether lack benevolence and still be an unqualifiedly good person is not plausible. Why, though, is it not enough, in order to be a good person, to be firmly determined to be guided by the relevant norms of action, the norms that determine what is right? A just person lacking benevolence might adopt the precept of acting as a kind person would act. It might be that such a person would lack a certain sensitivity to the needs of others, a sensitivity that is a component of virtues of benevolence, and this might result in some missed opportunities to act kindly. Still, though, it is not all that difficult to work out what a kind person would do in most situations.

The phenomena of benevolence and justice tend to be complex. Discussing what he calls "moral perception," Lawrence Blum makes the point that sensitivity to moral aspects of situations "involves multifarious moral and psychological processes" (1994, 31). His examples illustrate the point that kind individuals vary in their sensitivity to the well-being of different categories of people and in their sensitivity to different sorts of harms to people—physical pain, depression, humiliation, and the like. So one person might be keenly aware of the distress of children but not of adults, while another might be sensitive to others' physical comfort but not to the feelings of racial minorities (46–48).

We can add further complications to Blum's list. In particular situations, people tend to notice the sorts of things that they care about. People who are kind care about the well-being of others, and thus they tend to notice how others are faring. People of cold temperament, lacking in kindness, who think they should act as kind people do, could also cultivate a tendency to pay attention to others' weal and woe. They attend to others' welfare because they think it is right to do so. "I think I should act as kind people do, so I will be on the lookout for opportunities so to act." Such individuals might generally act as kind people act, but in so acting, they would not be expressing the feeling toward others of genuinely kind people. Of course, acting for this reason as kind people act might eventually lead to the acquisition of a genuine concern for others' well-being.

Just people are committed quite generally to acting as they should in moral matters. Why do we suppose that it is important as well to possess a sympathetic concern for others, especially in view of the frequency with which sympathetic impulses *conflict* with the indications of norms? What is the particular contribution of benevolence to good character?

David Hume went some distance in explaining the need for both benevolence and justice in good character. His ethical theory also provides an explanation of why these virtues tend to conflict.

Morality, Hume claimed, is internally connected with our deepest concerns, with matters that are central to needs and interests that we all have. "The social virtues of humanity and benevolence," he said in *An Enquiry Concerning the Principles of Morals,* "exert their influence immediately, by a direct tendency or instinct, which chiefly keeps in view the simple object, moving the affections, and comprehends not any scheme or system, nor the consequences resulting from the concurrence, imitation, or example of others" (1751, 93). Acting kindly because so doing fulfills an important need of another or advances the interest of another, simply because one cares about that person's welfare, is acting in a way that expresses the trait benevolence. The act is aimed by the agent directly at another's good. We all tend to value benevolent acts; we identify with the people who are the beneficiaries of such acts. In the absence of interfering considerations, we tend to be glad for the recipient and approving of the agent. That the trait benevolence is a virtue, Hume says, is explained by the fact that it is found universally to be both useful (in promoting our important needs and interests) and agreeable (1751, 16–20, 66–68).

Hume contrasts acts that express "the social virtues of justice and fidelity" with benevolent acts. The former virtues are "absolutely necessary to the well-being of mankind," he says, but the benefit of them "is not the consequence of every individual single act." A single act of justice may have "pernicious consequences." Rather, the benefit of virtues of justice "arises from the whole scheme or system, concurred in by the whole, or the greater part of society." There is no way, Hume claims, to realize the benefit of the "whole scheme" without bad consequences in some cases. "General inflexible rules [are] necessary to support general peace and order in society....Though such rules are adopted as best serve the same end of public utility, it is impossible for them to prevent all particular hardships, or make beneficial consequences result from every individual case" (Hume 1751, 93–94).

The rules of justice are artifacts, on Hume's view. They are instruments people employ for certain purposes—purposes that are connected with needs and interests central to our well-being. The rules are useful. The virtue justice involves an acceptance of and a willingness to observe certain of these rules: his favorite examples are the norms of property, promising, and government. Since the rules in question are artifacts, the creations of human beings, in *A Treatise of Human Nature* Hume calls justice an "artificial" virtue (1839–40, 477, 496–497). The virtue is essentially an individual's disposition toward certain artifacts—an acceptance of the authority of the rules and a commitment to follow them. Without the artifacts, this virtue could not exist. These are special artifacts, however. They consist of rules, and their existence depends entirely upon the fact that there is general understanding of them and an acknowledgment of their authority. Benevolence, on the other hand, is a "natural" virtue. It is based upon a tendency that people have by nature, and it requires no particular artifacts for its existence as justice does.

According to Hume's account, justice and benevolence will conflict on some occasions. When a rule of justice requires an act that has "pernicious consequences" for some individual(s), justice will prompt the action, but, presumably, benevolence will oppose it. One might suppose that the existence of such conflicts shows that the rules of justice require revision, but this is not Hume's view. The need for the system of rules that define the institution of property, Hume argues, is the need for a peaceful way to resolve the conflicts of interest between people when more than one individual wants the same material good. Because of the moderate scarcity of the material things people need and desire, such conflicts are inevitable, and a generally accepted scheme for resolving such conflicts of interest promotes security and social harmony. The resulting peace and security of possession provide incentives for production of goods and a condition for fruitful cooperation among people. Because of the nature of the circumstances that call for such a scheme, however, no scheme could guarantee that every party's desires will be satisfied on every occasion. It is not possible to satisfy fully every particular claim based upon need or interest. The resolution of a particular conflict of interests in a way that satisfies the interest of one party would likely frustrate and disappoint another party. It is possible that in particular cases, the action indicated by the rules will on the particular occasion produce more harm than good. Because of the nature of the rules and the purpose that it is their function to serve, those who accept the rules must be willing sometimes to forgo their own interests when the rules so indicate and to see others from time to time lose under the rules as well (Hume 1739–40, 497–8).

Notice, though, that on Hume's view, the whole point of the practice composed of rules that sometimes indicate acts that will harm people is "the public interest." "Public utility is the *sole* origin of justice, and…reflections on the beneficial consequences of this virtue are the *sole* foundation of its merit" (Hume 1751, 20). People who were not keenly interested in the welfare of people generally would not have such social artifacts.

Hume is sometimes thought to be defending a version of "rule utilitarianism" in his account of justice. The word "utility" figures prominently in Hume's argument, but it does not have the meaning that Bentham later gave it, where it is thought of as a single, homogeneous, quantifiable thing that enlightened people strive always to maximize. For Hume, utility is a synonym for usefulness. When Hume speaks of the utility of rules, he means their usefulness to people and communities for quite specific purposes. Rules, norms, have utility for Hume in exactly the sense that the tools in a toolbox do. It helps in understanding and appreciating his account of justice not to think of him as any sort of utilitarian.

Hume's account explains in a plausible way why a person who is both just and benevolent is likely to encounter circumstances in which one virtue prompts the person to one course of action and the other virtue to a contrary action. If Hume is right, such conflicts between benevolence and justice are not eliminable. What Hume thinks one should do in circumstances where justice and benevolence are in conflict is not clear. Sometimes, he seems to endorse the position that one should in every such case follow the rules of justice. He does allow, however, that the rules of justice are properly suspended in an emergency—in times of famine, the granaries are thrown open; in a shipwreck, one properly seizes any object that will keep one afloat without worrying about the rights of the owner of the object, and so on (Hume 1751, 22–23). Would Hume accept the possibility, though, that justice might on occasion properly be tempered with mercy even though no catastrophe threatened, even though the rules of justice are not "suspended"? This part of Hume's account is not developed.

Hume conceived the norms of justice as rules that constitute property, promising, and government. He explained why these rules regularly require people to act contrary to their own interests and contrary to the interests of others, thus accounting for the conflicts of justice with self-interest and with benevolence. This is plausible, as far as it goes. It is important to notice, however, that the rules of property, promising, and government are not the only norms that conflict in this way with benevolence. A wide variety of rules, principles, precepts, and instructions—some clear candidates for the category "moral" and others not—occasion such conflicts.

Plato's illuminating view of community in the *Republic* is useful for exploring the relationship among the norms of practices, sociality, and individual character. Communities organized on the basis of a division of labor and specialization properly foster the development of bodies of practical knowledge based upon the experience of practitioners with specific useful tasks. People who specialize in building, agriculture, inquiry, law, healing, teaching, and the like, master a body of practical knowledge that contains the distillation of the experience of many others who have practiced the activity.

They receive this shared knowledge, practice it, add their bit to it, and communicate it to other practitioners.

These bodies of practical knowledge that we practice as specialists are social artifacts, too. They are also complexes of norms. What a specialist knows and practices is how to proceed so that tasks are done well rather than badly. The norms themselves, of course, reflect the experience of many individual practitioners: what they have learned about how to proceed in various circumstances so that the activity will actually serve the particular interest that is its reason for being. Among the norms that guide the participants in a particular practice are technical instructions that pertain to the task of producing such and such a result—a durable pot, a habitable shelter, an illuminating explanation, the reduction of a fever. Some of the relevant norms, however, are classified as ethical: certain tasks cannot go forward unless workers communicate truthfully with one another, unless individuals can be trusted to do what they say they will do, unless they trust one another not to harm them, and so on. Among the norms that constitute a body of practical knowledge such as medicine or agriculture are ethical norms.

Plato was concerned that a community organized according to the principle of division of labor and specialization be so structured that it promotes the simultaneous harmonious pursuit of these various specialized activities. A community that succeeds to an appreciable extent in fostering these activities and promoting their harmonious and effective practice Plato called a just community (433a–434e, 1992, 108–9). The aim, here, is the simultaneous effective practice of many different activities that contribute in various important ways to the satisfaction of people's needs and interests with a minimum of conflict and interference with one another. It would be even better, of course, if each of the activities was practiced in ways that sustained and advanced the effective practice of *other* activities. The community would then be a system of harmonious and mutually reinforcing activities that serve an expanding variety of important needs and interests. The different activities would be practiced in a way that reflects their *adjustment* to one another. To realize this aim, the practitioners of the various special activities must not only be guided by norms that indicate how the purpose of their particular activity is to be attained, but they must as well practice their activities in ways that do not interfere with and that even foster the practice of other important activities.

Among the norms that constitute bodies of practical knowledge such as agriculture, sculpture, and navigation, then, are norms that indicate the right way to proceed in order to attain the purpose that defines the practice *and* other norms that indicate how the practice is to be performed in such a way that it harmonizes with and supports other important practices. The norms of various activities, then, will reflect the current knowledge of how things should be done in order to realize the activities' own purposes, but they will also reflect the presence of other activities in their adaptation and adjustment to them. The activities pursued simultaneously in the same community in varying degrees "interpenetrate" (Dewey's term). It is worth noting, too, that among the norms of an activity that serve to harmonize its practice with the practice of other activities are some Humean "rules" of justice—rules of property, promising, and government.

At the beginning of *Politics*, Aristotle announced that the way to study community is to go back to its beginnings and trace its growth (1252a 25–26, 1998, 2). People live together because individuals are not self-sufficient. They cannot on their own provide even the bare necessities of life, but while "[the community] comes to be for the sake of living,…it remains in existence for the sake of living well" (1252b 28–29, 1998, 3). This remark is made, presumably, with Plato's account of community organized on the principle of division of labor and specialization in mind. Good living for human beings, according to Aristotle, is activity that exhibits excellences of thought and character—virtues (*Nicomachean Ethics* 1098a 16–18, 1999, 9). The activity that exhibits excellences, of course, includes activity that is done well in accordance with the appropriate standards or norms.

Community, conceived in Plato's way as a means for making human beings more self-sufficient by providing them with food, shelter, and security, is also the occasion, the matrix, for creating complex activities rich with norms and standards. These activities and the standards for doing them well are related to people's needs and desires for food, shelter, security, and so on, but once the activities develop in a complex community, the interests that occasioned them develop and multiply (Dewey 1922, 56–57, MacIntyre 1984, 189–90). The developed activities become in themselves objects of intense interest and appreciation. A good life is not merely a life of subsistence; it involves absorption in useful complex activities that require practical knowledge for their performance. The acquired, refined capacities and dispositions that individuals need in order to participate successfully in these activities are excellences of thought and character—skills, know-how, and virtues of character. Not only is community necessary, then, for providing the necessities for human existence, but sociality also provides a necessary condition for developed practical knowledge, cultivated know-how, and technical and ethical norms. These things provide the basis for lives. Living well, as Aristotle said, is more than merely securing the necessities for sustaining life; it is a matter of doing well in cultivated practices in accordance with pertinent standards.

Complex activities that obviously serve the purposes of various cultivated human needs and interests are themselves objects of intense interest and cultivation—they themselves are central constituents in living well. Fortunate people are able to flourish in activities they love. Obviously, we do not value such activities only instrumentally. Community, which repairs our lack of individual self-sufficiency, makes possible the knowledge of good and bad and, of course, activity in accordance with such knowledge. Central to such activity is observing standards, following technical and moral norms.

Sociality, living together and sharing a highly structured way of life, is obviously necessary for complex activities, and in that sense it is a condition for survival *and* for good living. This indicates its importance. At the same time, sociality, like cultivated complex activities, is itself a focus of intense interest and appreciation. As we participate together in many activities, we value our associates and our association with them, and we do not value them only as instruments. Such associations are, in themselves, a possible source of deep satisfaction and, as Aristotle saw (*Nicomachean Ethics* 1097b10, 1999, 8), an important component of living well. Friendship, affection, love, fellow-feeling, and solidarity are refinements of this appreciation of those with whom we share our lives. People are associates, actual and potential. Benevolence can be viewed as the perfection of our appreciation of one another, of us who are together in community a sine qua non condition of good human life and of satisfaction in living it. It is an appreciation that is expressed in active concern for that association and for the good of other individuals who are our partners in living such a life. It belongs, though, to a form of life that is also thoroughly structured by technical and ethical norms.

It is *our* needs and interests that are so obviously served by the existence of the community; *we* are the beneficiaries of the division of labor and the cultivation of bodies of practical knowledge and the efforts to coordinate and harmonize the simultaneous pursuit of these myriad activities. We benefit from the "utility" (in Hume's sense) of a great variety of social artifacts, including the social artifacts Hume called justice. For our benefit, the norms that guide these matters are shaped.

There are, of course, at any time certain worthwhile things that we are unable to do, and certain important problems that we cannot solve. Our activities and practices, obviously, are flawed, nor can they be adequate as they stand for the hitherto unprecedented problems that continually confront us in a changing world. Human communities exist precariously in a world of discord and brutality.

In the end, the improvement, refinement, reformation, and adaptation of practice is possible only with an eye to our many and varied needs and interests. We are quite right to reject the idea that justice without benevolence might suffice for good character. Much of the point of justice would be opaque to us if we lacked the concern and fellow-feeling of which benevolence is the perfection; we as individuals would be hampered in our ability to think critically and constructively about issues of justice and norm-governed action generally without an appreciation of *our* stake in the matter, without an appreciation of *us*.

We, as individuals, with some frequency encounter situations in which benevolence indicates one course of action and justice a contrary one. What help can the foregoing reflections offer to an individual confronted by such a problem? Following a central insight of Plato's *Republic*, we can think of such problems as reflections in the psyches of individual human beings of the problems of a community in harmonizing the simultaneous cultivation and pursuit of a great variety of activities and related concerns. Activities and the norms that guide people in their practice exist only insofar as individuals master the requisite shared practical knowledge and practice it. The locus of these norms is to be found in the skills, knowhow, dispositions, and concerns of individuals. An individual can practice a complex activity only if these capacities and dispositions are so adjusted to one another that they operate harmoniously and express themselves in "a unified course of action." "Interpenetration of habits" was Dewey's term for this adjustment to one another of individuals' psychical dispositions needed to practice effectively complex activities. This adjustment is character (Dewey 1922, 29). In their cultivation of just a few activities, people encounter the problem of following simultaneously the many technical and moral norms that constitute their activities in accordance with their many concerns. These matters conflict again and again—because of their nature and because of complexity and change. Insofar as individuals are able to find ways to follow these norms simultaneously in ways that advance their concerns, they mirror the community's mission of harmonization, and they may contribute to the mission.

One thing that individuals properly strive to do is to pursue a complex activity in a way that reflects their concern for the happiness and welfare of others. At first glance, it seems hopeless: teachers must disappoint certain students with stringent criticism of their work, or they must give undeserved praise, which is unfair and bad pedagogy. One cannot, it seems, be both just and benevolent. This account, however, is superficial. If the pedagogy is well conceived and properly executed, the teachers' criticism can in the end benefit the students. This is a matter of the health of the practice of teaching and the mastery of it by individual teachers. Nor are teachers required to harden their hearts in criticizing students and forget about the students' immediate discomfort. Criticism often can be delivered in a way that says convincingly, "I want you to improve because I care about you, and I am going to help you." A teacher who offers pedagogically well-conceived criticism in this manner and then delivers on the promise of help is effectively harmonizing benevolence, justice, and pedagogical art. The adverse criticism, properly delivered, can effectively express concern for students' welfare. Every teacher recognizes that this is good pedagogy and realizes, too, that this is often very difficult to do. There are, of course, circumstances where it is just not possible to harmonize these things very well. The art of teaching, however, involves dealing with all these matters. These patterns recur, over and over, with variations in other activities (Dewey 1922, 132–53).

For individuals in particular situations, the ways in which benevolence may conflict with moral and other norms are uncountable. The aim of harmonizing these norms and values in conflict will have to be sought in every case with an eye to what the particular circumstances will permit. Tuition in this sort of task—harmonizing conflicting norms and related concerns—is best conceived as a part of instruction in one or more of the activities that make up our lives. The observance of ethical norms is indispensable for the proper performance of the activities that constitute our lives. The shape and the purpose of these norms is determined by their place in these activities. The norms themselves reflect their role in activities. Understanding them is properly a matter of understanding how they, together with other norms, contribute to the practice of these activities. The effort to teach ethics as an autonomous subject, abstracted from the particular complex activities that constitute our lives, actually distorts the ideas of these values and norms. It encourages those who think that ethics in everyday life is optional, an embellishment on our practice that, while it might be nice and sometimes expeditious, is really dispensable.

The virtues of justice and benevolence are the perfection of capacities and dispositions that are indispensable to the sorts of activities to which people dedicate their lives. The activities are inconceivable without them. Technical considerations, moral norms, and a complex appreciation of the importance of needs and interests of people "interpenetrate" in complex practices. The corresponding dispositions, Deweyan habits, in individuals who have mastered these activities, their skills, know-how, valuings, and commitments likewise interpenetrate, and this, Dewey points out, is what we call character. These traits in a well-integrated character are so related that they can, in a wide range of circumstances, be expressed simultaneously. They even support and reinforce one another, as a skilled teacher's benevolent concern for the welfare of students and cultivated ability to impart effective criticism are mutually reinforcing. Even the best-integrated character, however, cannot avoid circumstances that bring its constituent "habits" into conflict with one another.

In expressing Plato's ideal of the unity of the virtues, McDowell overstates an important point. "We cannot disentangle genuine possession of kindness from the sensitivity which constitutes fairness. And since there are obviously no limits on the possibilities for compresence, in the same situation, of circumstances of the sorts proper sensitivities to which constitute all the virtues, the argument can be generalized: no one virtue can be fully possessed except by a possessor of all of them, that is, a possessor of virtue in general" (McDowell 1998, 53).

The thesis that an individual cannot possess a virtue such as kindness without possessing all the other virtues is mistaken. There is, however, a deeper, more complex relationship between benevolence and justice; they are in an important way implicated in one another, even as they come into conflict. Virtues of benevolence are the perfection of the concern for one another that gives virtues of justice their point. Berlin and Hume are right, because conflict between these virtues is over-determined and inescapable. Dewey's point is that in a person of good character, the conflict between these virtues is softened, and they are made to support one another. A person's continual struggle to harmonize these competing tendencies is Dewey's version of the Socratic mission of tending the soul.

Bibliography

Aristotle. 1928. *Metaphysics*, 2d ed. Translated by W. D. Ross in *The Works of Aristotle Translated into English*, vol. 8. Oxford: Clarendon Press.

——. 1998. *Politics.* Translated by C. D. C. Reeve. Indianapolis, Ind.: Hackett.

——. 1999. *Nicomachean Ethics*, 2d ed. Translated by T. Irwin. Indianapolis, Ind.: Hackett.

Arras, J. D. 1991. "Getting Down to Cases: The Revival of Casuistry in Bioethics." *Journal of Medicine and Philosophy* 16:21–59.

Baron, M. W. 1995. *Kantian Ethics Almost without Apology.* Ithaca, N.Y.: Cornell University Press.

Benjamin, M. 2003. *Philosophy and This Actual World.* Lanham, Md.: Rowman and Littlefield.

Berlin, I. 1988. "The Pursuit of the Ideal." Reprinted in Berlin 1992.

——. 1992. *The Crooked Timber of Humanity.* Edited by Henry Hardy. New York: Vintage Books.

Blum, L. A. 1994. *Moral Perception and Particularity.* Cambridge: Cambridge University Press.

Brandt, R. B. 1976. "The Psychology of Benevolence." *Journal of Philosophy* 73: 429–53.

Butterfield, H. 1965. *The Origins of Modern Science*, rev. ed. New York: Free Press.

Cohen, J. 1986. Review of Michael Walzer, *Spheres of Justice. Journal of Philosophy* 83:457–68.

Cranston, M. 1991. "John Locke and the Case for Toleration." In Horton and Mendus 1991, 78–97.

Daniels, N. 1996. *Justice and Justification: Reflective Equilibrium in Theory and Practice.* Cambridge: Cambridge University Press.

Bibliography

Dancy, J. 1993. *Moral Reasons*. Oxford: Blackwell.

———. 2004. *Ethics without Principles*. Oxford: Clarendon Press.

Dewey, J. 1920. *Reconstruction in Philosophy*. In *John Dewey: The Middle Works, 1899–1924*, vol. 12. Edited by J.-A. Boydston. Carbondale: Southern Illinois University Press, 1988.

———. 1922. *Human Nature and Conduct*. In *John Dewey: The Middle Works, 1899–1924*, vol. 14. Edited by J.-A. Boydston. Carbondale: Southern Illinois University Press, 1983.

———. 1927. *The Public and Its Problems*. In *John Dewey: The Later Works, 1925–1953*, vol. 2. Edited by J.-A. Boydston. Carbondale: Southern Illinois University Press, 1988.

Dworkin, R. 1986. *Law's Empire*. Cambridge, Mass.: Harvard University Press.

———. 1993. *Life's Dominion: An Argument about Abortion, Euthanasia, and Individual Freedom*. New York: Alfred A. Knopf.

Ebbs, G. 1997. *Rule-Following and Realism*. Cambridge, Mass.: Harvard University Press.

Elgin, C. Z. 1991. "Understanding: Art and Science." In French, Uehling, and Wettstein 1991, 196–208.

Finnis, J. 1980. *Natural Law and Natural Rights*. Oxford: Clarendon Press.

French, P., T. E. Uehling, Jr., and H. K. Wettstein, eds. 1991. *Midwest Studies in Philosophy*, vol. 16: *Philosophy and the Arts*. Notre Dame, Ind.: University of Notre Dame Press.

Goodman, N. 1968. *Languages of Art*. Indianapolis, Ind.: Bobbs-Merrill.

Gough, J. W. 1991. "The Development of Locke's Belief in Toleration." In Horton and Mendus 1991, 57–77.

Hare, R. M. 1967. "Philosophical Discoveries." In Rorty 1967, 206–17.

Hart, H. L. A. 1961. *The Concept of Law*. Oxford: Clarendon Press.

Hill, C. 1961, 1980. *The Century of Revolution, 1603–1714*, 2d ed. New York: W. W. Norton.

Hooker, B., and M. Little. 2000. *Moral Particularism*. Oxford: Clarendon Press.

Horton, J., and S. Mendus, eds. 1991. *John Locke: A Letter Concerning Toleration in Focus*. London: Routledge.

Hume, D. 1739–40. *A Treatise of Human Nature*. Edited by L. A. Selby-Bigge, 2d ed. revised 1978 by P. H. Nidditch. Oxford: Clarendon Press.

———. 1751. *An Enquiry Concerning the Principles of Morals*. Edited by J. B. Schneewind. Indianapolis, Ind.: Hackett.

Hursthouse, R. 1999. *On Virtue Ethics*. Oxford: Oxford University Press.

Irwin, T. H. 2000. "Ethics as an Inexact Science: Aristotle's Ambitions for Moral Theory." In Hooker and Little 2000, 100–129.

Jacobson, D. 2005. "Seeing by Feeling: Virtues, Skills, and Moral Perception." *Ethical Theory and Moral Practice* 8:387–409.

Jonsen, A. R., and S. Toulmin. 1988. *The Abuse of Casuistry: A History of Moral Reasoning.* Berkeley: University of California Press.

Kant, I. 1785. *Grundlegung zur Metaphysik dur Sitten (Grounding for the Metaphysics of Morals).* Translated by James W. Ellington. Indianapolis, Ind.: Hackett, 1981.

———. 1797. *Metaphysik der Sitten (The Metaphysics of Morals).* Translated and edited by Mary Gregor. Cambridge: Cambridge University Press, 1996.

Locke, J. 1689. *A Letter Concerning Toleration.* Edited by James H. Tully. Indianapolis, Ind.: Hackett, 1983.

———. 1690. *Second Treatise of Government.* Edited by C. D. Macpherson. Indianapolis, Ind.: Hackett, 1980.

MacIntyre, A. 1984. *After Virtue,* 2d ed. Notre Dame: University of Notre Dame Press.

McDowell, J. 1998. *Mind, Value, and Reality.* Cambridge, Mass.: Harvard University Press.

Mill, J. S. 1957. *Utilitarianism.* Indianapolis, Ind.: Bobbs-Merrill.

———. 1961. *A System of Logic,* 8th ed. London: Longmans, Green.

Montesquieu, C. 1748. *De l'Esprit des loix (The Spirit of the Laws).* In *Montesquieu: Selected Political Writings.* Edited and translated by M. Richter. Indianapolis, Ind.: Hackett, 1990.

Moody-Adams, M. M. 1997. *Fieldwork in Familiar Places: Morality, Culture, and Philosophy.* Cambridge, Mass.: Harvard University Press.

Murphy, A. E. 1964. *The Theory of Practical Reason.* LaSalle, Ill.: Open Court.

Nicholson, P. 1991. "John Locke's Later Letters on Toleration." In Horton and Mendus 1991, 163–87.

Nussbaum, M. C. 1990. *Love's Knowledge: Essays on Philosophy and Literature.* Oxford: Oxford University Press.

———. 2000. *Women and Human Development: The Capabilities Approach.* Cambridge: Cambridge University Press.

O'Neill, O. 1989. *Constructions of Reason: Explorations of Kant's Practical Philosophy.* Cambridge: Cambridge University Press.

Plato. 1953. *Parmenides.* Translated by B. Jowett in *The Dialogues of Plato,* 4th ed. vol. 2. Oxford: Clarendon Press.

———. 1992. *Republic.* Translated by G. M. A. Grube, revised by C. D. C. Reeve. Indianapolis, Ind.: Hackett.

Rawls, J. 1971, 1999. *A Theory of Justice,* rev. ed. Cambridge, Mass.: Harvard University Press.

———. 1993, 1996. *Political Liberalism.* New York: Columbia University Press.

Rorty, R., ed. 1967. *The Linguistic Turn: Recent Essays in Philosophical Method.* Chicago: University of Chicago Press.

Rorty, R. 1989. *Contingency, Irony, and Solidarity.* Cambridge: Cambridge University Press.

Ross, W. D. 1930. *The Right and the Good.* Oxford: Clarendon Press.

Scanlon, T. M. 1982. "Contractualism and Utilitarianism." In Sen and Williams 1982, 103–28.

———. 1998. *What We Owe to Each Other.* Cambridge, Mass.: Harvard University Press.

Sen, A., and B. Williams, eds. 1982. *Utilitarianism and Beyond.* Cambridge: Cambridge University Press.

Sidgwick, H. 1907. *The Methods of Ethics,* 7th ed. Chicago: University of Chicago Press.

Urmson, J. O. 1974–75. "A Defense of Intuitionism." *Proceedings of the Aristotelian Society* 75: 111–19.

Veyne, P. 1987. *From Pagan Rome to Byzantium.* In *A History of Private Life,* vol. 1. Edited by Paul Veyne, translated by Arthur Goldhammer. Cambridge, Mass.: Harvard University Press.

Waldron, J. 1991. "Locke: Toleration and the Rationality of Persecution." In Horton and Mendus 1991, 98–124.

Wallace, J. D. 1988. *Moral Relevance and Moral Conflict.* Ithaca, N.Y.: Cornell University Press.

———. 1996. *Ethical Norms, Particular Cases.* Ithaca, N.Y.: Cornell University Press.

Walzer, M. 1977. *Just and Unjust Wars: A Moral Argument with Historical Illustrations.* New York: Basic Books.

———. 1983. *Spheres of Justice.* New York: Basic Books.

———. 1987. *Interpretation and Social Criticism.* Cambridge, Mass.: Harvard University Press.

———. 1994. *Thick and Thin: Moral Argument at Home and Abroad.* Notre Dame, Ind.: University of Notre Dame Press.

Will, F. L. 1988. *Beyond Deduction: Ampliative Aspects of Philosophical Reflection.* New York: Routledge.

———. 1997. *Pragmatism and Realism.* Edited by K. R. Westphal. Lanham, Md.: Rowman and Littlefield.

Williams, B. 1985. *Ethics and the Limits of Philosophy.* Cambridge, Mass.: Harvard University Press.

———. 1993. *Shame and Necessity.* Berkeley: University of California Press.

———. 1995. *Making Sense of Humanity and Other Philosophical Papers.* Cambridge: Cambridge University Press.

Wittgenstein, L. 1953. *Philosophical Investigations.* Translated by G. E. M. Anscombe. New York: Macmillan.

Index